POLICE
CITIZEN
INTERACTION

SAM LUCKEY

CITIZEN
POLICE
INTERACTION

LET THE HEALING BEGIN

Every personal experience is "primed" by previous experience. Remain aware of the influence of "priming" on your personal and professional adventure here on Earth. I primed most paragraphs with a short "priming" phrase. Hopefully, I can help you develop a "positive" habit involving awareness and recognition of any "priming" effects infecting your here now behavior. Behavior is a property of the brain; we are social-creatures always being primed through social-interaction. **YOU HAVE BEEN PRIMED**

POLICING
P-R-I-V-A-T-E
PERSONALITIES

U.S. ARMY CID SPECIAL AGENT SAM LUCKEY

PRE-PROGRAMMING
POSITIVE-PROACTIVE
POLICE
PHENOMENON

POLICE COLD WAR

CID SPECIAL AGENT SAM LUCKEY

1950 IN THIS MEMORIAL 1953
ARE INSCRIBED THE NAMES OF MEN
FROM BRITAIN CANADA AUSTRALIA
NEW ZEALAND AND SOUTH AFRICA
WHO FELL IN THE KOREAN WAR
AND HAVE NO KNOWN GRAVE
DIED WITH MEN OF OTHER COUNTRIES
FIGHTING TO UPHOLD THE IDEALS
OF THE UNITED NATIONS

U.S. ARMY 1976-1987--OVER 250 PHOTOGRAPHS

MILITARY
POLICE
SCHOOL

HISTORICAL-EXPERIENCE-MEMORIES

Contents

INTRODUCTION

POLICE-CITIZEN INTERACTION: A police-officer intuits something is not right, but does not know why! "Subliminal-perception" or human abilities that cannot be documented to satisfy investigative science? Are we in control of "fear-reactions," or are we reacting with "fear"? Unconscious memories that you do not recognize or remember—past realizations out of your awareness, are influencing your behavior right now. An "event" requires that the police-officer determines "meaning," as we are the MEDIATION EXPERTS! Have you "refined" your "prediction-oriented-personality" police-skills?

CITIZEN-POLICE INTERACTION: Police-officers have to balance "occupational-tasks" with "societal-tasks," with "specific-community tasks," with "personal-tasks," and "family-tasks." Is your "real-self," even close to the "ideal-self" you imagine and empower? Do you ignore such choices and responsibilities, and just hope for the best? Human tendencies to choose good or bad may be more determined by neurochemical differences and fluctuations—than rational thought. Assumptions make our experience easier—not necessarily more accurate. Experts explain that without unconscious assumption mental processes, we would not understand the world around us. Most of our mental representations of the world are based on non-stop assumptions, bathed in undisciplined thoughts after thoughts after thoughts.

POLICE-CITIZEN INTERACTION: Police-officers graduate from simple "sensory-analysis" and have no choice but to become experts in "social-situational-analysis." Subjective analysis involves "inferences," judgments," "logically-related," "preventing harm" and many harder to define socio-cultural interpretations and expectations described as the most complex social skills humans possess. Your association skills concerning stimulus and response will be influenced by "reinforcing stimuli" and "punishing stimuli."

<u>CITIZEN-POLICE INTERACTION:</u> A SWAT police-officer, waiting around the corner to be part of a raid on a residence—in anticipation and a little anxiety—has to experience a little "imagination" for the waiting to become "anticipation." Otherwise, you are just waiting. Some neuroscientists theorize that all human perception skills require some form of imagination. To even be conscious we have to "imagine" that everything we cannot sense at that moment—still exists in "present-tense-awareness." Our brains have been called "anticipation-machines." We consciously console our unconscious. Think about this—we can change the way we think as we "neuronally-probe" what is outside our skin.

ALL POLICE-CITIZEN INTERACTION AND CITIZEN-POLICE INTERACTION IS HEAVILY INFLUENCED BY "**PRIMING**" JUST PRIOR TO THE INTERACTION. BE AWARE OF THIS "**PRIMING**" INFLUENCE ON YOUR BEHAVIOR.

CHAPTER ONE
INVESTIGATIVE NARRATIVE DETAILS

Scientists investigating "meaningful-noises" that police-officers emit, describe language as a "system-of-behaviors" bathed in "hierarchal-structure" and cognitive conditioning. Human language behaviors are heavily influenced by interdependent anatomical and physiological relationships, hopefully flavored with emotional discipline when interacting with other humans. Language as symbolic substitutions for "concepts," like, "gun," "angry-spouse," or "take-cover." Language broke-down into, usually, but not always, mutually accepted "arbitrary conventions" as an aide for law-enforcement to communicate effectively with local citizenry. Occasionally, simply repeating what an emotional citizen speaks to you is enough to **de-escalate** a situation. Two-way effective communication for meeting needs, wants and goals, sauteed by our personal beliefs and pre-programmed judgments. Unfortunately, we usually have three, four or more citizens, demanding our attention-skills be focused on each one present, stressing and violating our "rule-governed" language system of behaviors.

"Language is not only symbolic, but the words we speak are just 'convenient noises.' Words should not be considered equivalent to direct actual 'experience, especially 'unmediated knowing.' There is a brief moment before words contaminate our direct experience (association and similarity), and ultimately, fraudulently, deceivingly, alter and influence memory processing, especially later recall." From POLICING PRIVATE PERSONALITIES SAM LUCKEY

SOCIAL-INTELLIGENCE NARRATIVE DETAILS

PATTERNS WITHIN PATTERNS

Advanced law-enforcement training may include improving your **"metalinguistic"** skills, using "language about language," and properly recognize and reflect on your own language comprehension skills. Experts describe that humans are born with "pattern-seeking bioprograms," sometimes referred to as "Universal-Grammar." The negative and the positive Documenting your investigative narrative-details will be more influenced by the mental-model you developed, than the actual reality of the situation. Limitations involving our language skills, voiced words-as-choices revealing "patterns-of-patterns," will be reflected in your citizen-interaction, especially attempts in de-escalation techniques. Language helps with our powers of foresight. Our social-intelligence includes the capability to deceive, and the capability to detect deception. <u>We should not be limited to "literal and immediate" perception</u>! Police-work requires creative, imaginative, figurative and intuitive mental processes working alongside "just-the-fact" perceptual categorization. Self-conscious awareness and attention are empowered through the use of language. Do you require language-based thoughts to practice a form of "mind-control" called "concentration."

"Experts remind us that the words we use do not actually carry meaning. The cognitive experience the receiver interprets of those same words 'evoke-meaning.' To clearly communicate our thinking to others and verify they properly understood our 'meaning,' requires 'others' to communicate clearly, their thinking back at us. Even 'signs' do not carry meaning. The receiver/observer 'evokes meaning,' and pattern recognition, a 'construing' interpretation and prediction process." From POLICING PRIVATE PERSONALITIES, SAM LUCKEY

CONTEXT CREATES DEFAULT MEANINGS

The assumptions a police-officer carries in his or her head upon arriving at a situation, will auto-infect your investigative style and auto-infect your conclusions. During police-citizen interaction, both parties are trying to re-create their version/mental-model of the situation into each other's mind, divergent thinking. When I managed a group-home for developmentally disabled children, I detected details involving our teaching-methods for understanding and speaking sign-language. It was much easier to teach the physical movement for particular "signs," than guaranteeing they really understood (**comprehension) what the signs** signified as social-tools. One resident with "down-syndrome," eagerly learned three signs, and refused to learn any more, that was all he needed. Signs for "coffee," "bed-time," and "more" during meals. Comprehension and production are two different mental processes. Experts declare that "context creates default meanings," especially when faced with environmental incoherence and novel situations that police-officers experience every day.

"Your 'beliefs' about the situation you're responding to, will motivate your behavior more than the actual situation. Your 'beliefs' can lead you astray and get you into serious trouble. 'Beliefs' can be a barrier between you and the actual reality of the situation. False beliefs do not magically disappear from memory. False beliefs may be out of your conscious awareness—but their influence can still remain, powerfully influencing your behavior. Some experts describe your 'emotional-response' as habitual, not as situational-specific and optimal as we would like to believe. Habits do not require 'thoughts-of-intent' to materialize and influence your life. Every habit of yours that you ignore and hope nobody else notices, 'creates an unconscious-expectation.' Every habit of yours is a 'filter,' between you and your experience." From POLICING PRIVATE PERSONALITIES, SAM LUCKEY

CULTURE INFLUENCES YOUR SENSE-OF-SELF

When you find your unconscious generating behaviors you did not consciously intend; your conscious thought processes try to "narrate" justification to yourself, and make sense of these behaviors—after the fact. You will use language to try to internally make a reasonable explanation for your behavior. Even if your "reasoning-skills" use false premises and false narratives to explain questionable behavior, you will not just believe your "reason" to be true, you will energetically and righteously defend your reason. Were you merely "induced" into questionable behavior by others? The influence of your unconscious on your speaking skills is absolute. From the words that reach conscious awareness and expression, to the motor programming required for proper "meaningful-noises" to be formed manipulating your lips, tongue, mouth and properly inhaling and exhaling. Neuroscientists have proven that your "reactions" to your environment do not only rely on conscious intended awareness. Neuroscientist Michael Persinger introduced the "**God Helmet**" to the world. Your ride while wearing the God Helmet is clearly influenced, if not determined by **cultural influence**. Dr. Persinger has taken "magnetic-fields" well beyond what our childhood may have accustomed us to. Electromagnets producing "temporal-lobe-transients" of instability; intentionally creating "microseizure" disruptions involving neuronal-firing patterns, altering your "**sense-of-self**" and suspending your cherished "**theories-of-mind**" beliefs! Subjects wearing the God Helmet routinely experience out-of-body-experiences, conversations with gods, angels and imaginary beings, even invisible presences that the subject can not explain.

I was dismayed and embarrassed when U.S. Supreme-court justice Antonio Scalia revealed to the world that he did not understand why God did not talk to believers as much as God had spoken in ancient times. He confirmed that he believed that hundreds of devils and Satan-characters walked amongst-us. I wish he could have been afforded the opportunity to wear a God Helmet, and see where such illusionary-religious beliefs really originate. In my 2nd book, Policing Private Personalities, I explain in more detail, neuroscientific investigations into the functional-role our brains (L) hemisphere processes, compared to the (R) hemisphere. Evolution has afforded our (L) hemisphere the mental-process recognized as our **"sense-of-self."** Micro-seizures in your temporal-lobe interfere with normal (L) and (R) hemispheric team-work. When the (L) hemisphere recognizes **"uncoordinated-activity,"** that it does not recognize as mere (R) hemisphere normal accompanied processes; cultural-influence sends the (L) hemisphere in search of any sensory-**perceptual-clarification** to help regain control, even illusory control. Any imaginary illusion that pops into your head, will be allowed conscious awareness and subsequent holy-amazement. You believe the illusion as fact, as, you are an impeccable and non-impeachable witness! You know when you lie and imagine, and this was neither. You will believe (role-play) God is talking to you, and all your other paranormal, imaginary friends and beliefs you were culturally (experience) indoctrinated into.

AUTOMATIC LEARNED EMOTIONAL RESPONSES

REPEAT-REPEAT-REPEAT-RETREAT

AUTOMATIC LEARNED EMOTIONAL RESPONSES

Are you alert enough to recognize when your brain chemistry and electrical-activity has been slightly altered? It is easier to recognize when our respiration rate has been altered, or when we feel like we are about to pass-out. Your brain can have injuries you are totally unaware of. Others in your life may identify your mental-dysfunction before you recognize cognitive defects in yourself. Michael Shermer described his experience wearing the God Helmet as a "tug-of-war between the **rational and emotional parts** of his brain." Stimulate (legally) your temporal-lobe someday, see what you experience—the "sensed-presence-effect." Which auto-response was chosen for you, from your library of learned-**emotional responses**? Humans are amygdala fear-based motivated and stimulated social-creatures, who expect the presence of others (mind-extension?), even if we have to imagine them. Automatic emotional responses do not mean they are "controlled" and

7

actually helpful, responses—or even fulfill long-term self-interest planning expectations. Self and other, the easiest of all social-deterministic beliefs we possess. Yet, damage to your posterior superior parietal lobe may influence your ability to determine self from other, even disrupt neuronal imaging that informationally identifies/recognizes your body as object, position and location in our social-environment.

On my 4th overseas tour with the Army, in West Germany, I was a CID Special Agent. I had to interview a witness at a Camp in West Germany that I had never been to before. After the interview, I felt a nagging-pulling to an area that I could not resist. If I was on routine-patrol, I would have immediately intuited something was wrong or needed my attention and headed in that direction. I was done for the day, and had a long drive back to Frankfurt, so I just kind of ended up at an area with more **warning signs, multiple fence-lines and antennas** than I saw when I guarded nuclear weapons. I stopped short of the facility, armed, wearing my "detective" civilian suit and carrying my briefcase. I was effortlessly allowing my unconscious to analyze what I was seeing, not alarmed or concerned. Just curious why I was drawn to this facility that was originally out of my view? A soldier approaching the facility, nodded at me and asked if I had an appointment. I said no, admitting that I had no idea why I was drawn to such a facility? The soldier said, something like, oh! "They are going to love that!" I suspected it was a Military Intelligence or Counter Intelligence facility, this was during the Cold-War. Just a few hours from Soviet-bloc communist armies. After watching the movie, The Men Who Stare at Goats— was this part of the psychic spy program? If I was able to wear the God Helmet immediately, while still confused about what attracted me to that facility, what would I have imagined? A book on the subject described Army methods that <u>distracted your conscious awareness</u>, which allowed the power of your unconscious to extract-information from all the noise in the world.

8

SPECIES-SPECIFIC POLICE-SPECIFIC

PRE-PROGRAMMED INTERPRETATION

Language allows the police-officer just arriving at the scene of a complicated situation, to learn beyond present-situation socio-cultural environmental stimuli that they can see and verify for themselves. We "decode" utilizing our speech-perception skills, traits and acoustic cues, that are heavily influenced by all your prior conditioning and experience, more than the event itself. We can learn about events and concepts that are no-longer present, displaced, intentionally hidden, or just out of our sensory awareness. The less we respond as **pre-programmed robots**, the more successful our encounters will be. Effective communication involves pattern recognition that is "context dependent." Is everybody on the same page? Our pronouncement of words is naturally less precise, during conversation, than when we intentionally consciously ensure we say exactly what we mean. There is a theory that how we individually produce speech sounds, is the biggest influence on how we perceive "others" speech. Have you ever analyzed your "motor-speech-movements?" Motor commands are generated for speech. Your "species-specific" interpretation effort analyzing "speech signals" of others, are heavily influenced by your own "motor-speech-movements," all analyzed unconsciously, which steers and traps your conscious interpretation before you realize it. Intonation and "word-stress" is usually evident to a police-officer who is "**present with presence**," not a pre-programmed distracted robot. Near the end of our shift, if we morph into distracted day-dreaming police-officers, "present-without-presence" can get you killed. No police-officer has only "positive-traits." Understand your weaknesses and faults before someone else uses them against you. Recognize that your mind creates your reality, more than the reality of the situation you find yourself in. Right now, at this moment, what conversation is your "ego" having with itself? Is this conversation sending your mind and body in the direction you really want?

AMPLITUDE CAN DISGUISE INSECURITY

Every word you hear in routine conversation is processed out of your awareness, "lexical **ambiguity**," alongside every word that resembles it. "Syntactic **ambiguity**," hindering a citizens communication expression, may sound further ambiguous, related to "local **ambiguity**" and "standing **ambiguity**." What could go wrong? A "tip-of-the-tongue" mental-search experience at a critical moment, can damage your credibility when giving commands. Communicative competence is not only hard to teach a rookie, it can make or break one's career in law enforcement. Mental-grammar—your "internalized knowledge" when communicating with the outside world, requires an on-going mental processing involving you as "speaker" and you as "listener," at the same time. Then muscles that we rarely think of, get involved. Your "vocal-organs" have muscles. Then your "mind-as-speaker," interacts with a citizen "mind-of-the-listener." How do you express your thoughts or translate your thoughts into an expressed message? The process seems pretty automatic? We still do not really understand the "language of thought." We then speak immediate proper sentences without analysis, it just happens. Do you produce speech one word at a time? Do you speak utilizing "associative stimulus responses?" We do have a "Utterance Generator Model of Speech Production."

SUCCESSFUL COMMUNICATION SKILLS

Have you ever conducted a **"descriptive-linguistic"** personal investigation into your communication skills? Not the "prescriptive" rules we were taught in school, but exactly why you naturally utilize certain phrases or communicative mannerisms on a regular basis. Make a list of them. Are you proud of them all. Their effectiveness? Are your semantic "utterances" making sense to the citizenry we interact with on a daily basis? Are your utterances effective and productive? I found myself borrowing key words and phrases that I overheard other law-enforcement personnel utilize, that I liked and thought were effective. I tried hard, unsuccessfully, to not repeat, empower, spread or inherit out-of-control emotional phrases used regularly by those I patrolled alongside. Rookies can be taught "concepts" that should never have been described by a trainer or senior official, just like your own children. As responding pre-programmed robots, we are more likely to fail in successful communication skills; if we don't care enough to articulate exactly what is needed at that moment, or explain it in ambiguous ramblings because we are not sure what we intended to say. (Then we blame the citizen for not understanding what we were not sure of ourselves.) We were dispatched, we arrived, we spoke, fulfilling our service requirements for the community, indifferent if it really solved anything. Humans want to fill in the routine gaps of conversation, even if what is spoken is not pertinent or already discussed. We just seem to fulfill an ambiguous subconscious need—to keep the conversation going as part of our over-stimulated modern lifestyle. Amplitude can disguise insecurity, as well as a dominating and controlling attitude.

SUB-CONSCIOUS SPEECH PERCEPTION SKILLS

Your historical personal and professional experience, if you allow it; will define and limit your interpretation of events sub-consciously, before your conscious can make a proper diagnosis of the situation you find yourself in. You will usually not have a successful de-escalation dispatch, if you base your response and decision-making based primarily on **inferences and speculation**. Occasionally, after you solve or de-escalate an incident, sometimes we feel obligated to hang around and converse. Usually, this works out well, you feel good about your interaction. Sometimes, we stay a little longer, and a mistaken interpretation of something said sidetracks your success. Literal interpretation was determined when you were speaking "figuratively." How well do you remember what you do not

11

understand. Sometimes a police-officers "explanatory-talk" sounds more dominating and controlling than we really intended. You smile inside. You established meaning in your mind as you vocalize your de-escalation solutions; you quickly are reminded that "meaning" on the streets, has way more than "one-meaning" interpretive mental-dance. Spoken human speech is more complex than I ever imagined. Our conversational speech is believed to include 125-180 words per minute. Every second we process 25-30 phonetic segments. This proves how much of our speech perception skills are guided and energized by our subconscious. **Morphemes** are linguistic units of meaning, language at its smallest unit. Every morpheme is communicated by the speaker clearly and correctly, and every morpheme is received and understood exactly as the speaker intended. Good-luck on that one!

As a police officer gives instructions utilizing "meaningful noises," the receiver of those meaningful noises must employ sentence cognitive processing skills to determine meaning. When ordinary speech is analyzed using speech waveforms, scientist discovered that the waveforms lack what we are conditioned to believe we "hear," "breaks" between the words. It has been proven that what we believe we are hearing, isolated words, discrete segments with breaks in between words, is merely imposed by the listener. **"Meaning"** is determined by the whole sentence. During an emotionally challenging police-citizen discussion, the words we speak merge and blend while we compete for our voices to be heard. Human-tongues are required to "anticipate" articulating the vowel that follows a consonant, merging the previous sound with the slightly modified following consonant. Wave-form analysis will prove our speech is physically continuous, but our mind will perceive the conversation as a "sequence of discrete entities." This speech "discrete-segment" as a "theoretical-assumption," is heavily influenced by our phonological-description as an "artifact-of-analysis." Our personal articulatory and acoustic recognition mental skills manufacture the illusion of discrete-segmented assumptions. Our gift of written-language further ensnares our conversational assumptions, by providing written clear breaks, isolated words, and discrete segments. Written "graphic-symbols" in a sequence do not equate to spoken discrete segments.

BIASED PRE-PROGRAMMING

SITUATIONAL EVALUATION

Your vocal apparatus provides a continuous speech signal that automatically prepares for the next sound, slightly modifying in transition, the previous sound. If we had to consciously manipulate our tongue and lips for each word, we would sound pretty silly to each other. Language expert Sanford A. Schane describes language in a similar way that police-officers, in error, evolved to evaluate "**appearance versus reality.**" "In language the perceptual, the subjective, the discrete take precedence over the physical, the objective, the continuous." Our unconscious bias and pre-programming, if allowed, will evaluate the situation we responded to for us, potentially in conflict with the reality of the situation—potentially missing important breaks, isolated words and discrete segments important for clear understanding. Scientist found a clever way to clinically present one word at a time, instead of the whole sentence; which revealed **speech perception** clearly utilizes linguistic, semantic and syntactic context. A word edited out of a recorded sentence, and played back all alone for someone; revealed the word removed from the sentence, sometimes did not even sound like a word. Natural speech provides "automatic" unconscious processes. Spoken language is meaningless if the "meaningful-noises," or sounds we make, do not convey meaning. The meaning we intend is "manifested through sound."

Consider the following when evaluating your part in complicated **verbal emotional police-citizen interaction**; physical voice-anatomical differences, vocal-tract dissimilar shape contrasts involving opening and closing-constriction issues, timing issues, unclear intentions, dental-issues, poor verbal skills, superiority complex issues, sounds requiring aspirated or unaspirated stylistic variation, having over-confidence, or having no confidence in your public-speaking skills, interaction that requires speaking a second language, phonetic issues, spoken assimilatory processes, non-verbal body language differs from what is being expressed, cultural differences, racial differences, age differences, male/female issues, we individually rarely utter the same word-utterance identically as we just-uttered, distraction issues, safety issues, shift-almost-over issues, background marital problems, voice-quality and pitch at that time, weather conditions, interference from other citizens or even police, identical utterances may have different intended informational meaning, allophonic differences, voice inflection-stress and pitch issues, crowd issues, witnesses being critical, voice clarity and manners-of-articulation, abstract descriptions and representations, mandatory participation, phoneme variants, vowel-consonant dichotomy, you still have to monitor radio-traffic, the special-way we say certain syllables, the unconscious control of your tongue and lips when speaking, lax vowels, distinct tense vowels that may sound, in-error, as challenging or threatening, emotional residue hangover from a previous emotionally challenging dispatch, your past history with this particular citizen, or business or neighborhood, prosodic elements, intonation, effort, loudness issues, competing environmental sounds and other stimuli, affricates, fricatives or continuants, semivowels, nasal passage nasalization issues, total occlusion tongue effects, resonant properties—sonorants or obstruents, voiceless consonants, lexicon, glottalized consonants, phonetic parameters, body-of-tongue features and linguistic liberty! WHAT COULD GO WRONG?

"The order of our questions can be manipulated to guarantee that the first question, triggers an awareness in the suspect, that focuses

his or her mind, where we want their mind to be. Just because you have made a list of 20 prepared in advance questions for a particular suspect, that is not good enough. Look at your questions and know the order of questions that will guarantee your suspect will be focused where you want them. Social psychology has proven this to be effective, especially for police interviews. When interviewing citizens, law-enforcement finds that witnesses more easily remember what they 'heard,' over 'where' and 'whom.' Ideally, our witnesses thought processes operate from a more rational and 'cognitively logical' mindset. Be prepared for witnesses that seem to 'remember' from a more 'associatively illogical and irrational system of thinking.'" From POLICING PRIVATE PERSONALITIES SAM LUCKEY

CHAPTER TWO
<u>UNCONSCIOUS PRE-PROGRAMMED INTENTIONS</u>

Some police-officers are excellent at paying attention to the outside world, while neglecting "inner-attention focus," inner demons as **"internal adversaries."** Is your conscious experience of life merely an emotionally distracted roller coaster ride. Your undeclared and ill-defined intentions in life may contribute to the negativity you get back from the citizens you encounter, maybe even felt as the entire universe. It is better to "act" than merely "react." When expending energy to behaviorally "realize" what you (unconscious-conditioning) "desire," make sure that creates the environmental interactive feedback you really intended. We can activate movement from unconscious pre-programmed intentions—without sensory feedback, behavior that includes firing your weapon. Patrolling like a pre-programmed indifferent uncaring zombie, is the cognitive version of **"learned nonuse,"** normally attributed to limb-movement. Like the elderly family physician, who stops attending seminars and lectures on medical-advancements for a decade or more; police-officers may not be aware of how advanced neuro-sciences have become pertinent for law-enforcement. The health and welfare of the community and law-enforcement is awaiting your personal interest, research and on-the-job-use of modern science. Your association skills may result in a major advancement in police-sciences, beneficial for community and police. The Tyree Nichols incident in Memphis TN, where a group of police-officers were digitally recorded abusing Mr. Nichols, who died from those same injuries, and the camera was clearly present. If we are still committing horrors like that, then standard police-academy criteria have to be improved, if not overhauled. My memory of my first college course (1977) at Camp Ames Korea, was a class on Psychology for police and correctional officers. It seemed back then, that all we were taught was Freud, Jung, and Behaviorism.

UNIQUE-PERSONAL BIASED MENTAL PROPERTIES

Recognize and admit when feedback directed at you from family, friends and co-workers is best to act on, instead of waiting for community feedback and mandated control issues are directed at you. Make the right non-stop choice-after-choice-after choice, while learning from your mistakes. Sometimes, the "research" you conduct during routine-patrol, can be made more effective, if your "pre-conceptions" do not fixate on out-of-date behavior-patterns not pertinent at this here/now moment. Deepak Chopra describes that thoughts either exist as "memories or imaginings." Your law-enforcement "cognitive style" requires multiple aspects of attention and focus—countered by unconscious avoidance-conditioning-reinforcers so common in police-work. You can train yourself to be more successful at focusing attention, and improving your initial "breath of focus" when you initially scan and decipher what you have responded to. Training your focus of attention should include both internal and external based analysis. Unconscious undisciplined **fixation-of- attention** (usually just phenomena of your many habits), may lead you to consciously miss a cue something is wrong, or worse; undisciplined-fixation-of-attention has become a dangerous distraction. Consciousness, awareness and attention, experienced neuronally as images—may not be clearly defined thru your personal unique biased mental-properties. We just hope these cognitive processes are processed on normal mental pathways, out of your awareness, resulting in the truest interpretation of reality that you empowered. You can also use your fixation-of-attention skills to help prepare yourself (simulation) for responding to such emotional stimulation situations, and improving your confidence during these events.

UNCONSCIOUS REWARDS CENTER

MEANINGFUL COINCIDENCES

17

SUTRA: "I see the other in myself and myself in others." (The Mirror of Relationship.) Extrapolate what you can at these incidents, but you must keep your "extrapolations" reality-based, current and up-to-date. "Ignorance is constricted awareness. In order to notice something, you have to ignore everything else." Thought suppression sometimes fails because it still creates interest-thoughts during "active mental suppression," unintentionally motivating continuous intrusive associative thoughts; exposed to the world thru your body-language and non-verbal communication. Unconscious ambiguous inhibition attempts, may not be stronger than your ambiguous self-improvement attempts "meant-to-do-list." **"Intent creates coincidences."** Deepak Chopra may have not had law-enforcement in mind with this statement, but it sure is pertinent! When we "detect" coincidence in our lives, we are establishing some form of "meaning," indicating our "participation" in an event—meant coincidence. The message of the "coincidence" is felt as "meaning." Sometimes we recognize when we get what we deserve—subjective experience. Some consider "**synchronicity**" as more meaningful than mere-coincidence? Do not confuse habits and compulsions as meaningful-coincidences—that trigger your unconscious reward-centers as facts worth repeating. Automatic emotional behaviors have their purposes, just be aware when yours have no problem-solving helpful purpose for the specific here/now situation you were dispatched to. Refocusing is much easier in a classroom. All you have to do is be an "**impartial-participant**," which can be much harder than being an impartial-spectator. This is your cue—what do you do?

SELECTIVE ATTENTION—FIELD OF ATTENTION

Understand what is in your "**field-of-attention**." Humans have "selective-attention" skills that are never really trained or even recognized, so they atrophy into your worst subconscious habits involving citizen-interaction. Our physical interaction with other humans, vibrating at different electro-magnetic frequencies, vibrating humans interacting and bathing in each other's vibrating frequencies. Humans may feel the power of being the dominant animal on the planet right now, with all we know about the universe, but I believe we lost the most divine power we had long ago. The power to subconsciously recognize, decipher and transmit each other's Electro-Magnetic Field of information instantaneously and effortlessly. A few expert-physicists describe that 95% of the universe, cannot be described efficiently by our scientific earthbound laws. Your interaction with other humans is "framed," by your (**comfort zone**) personal prejudices and presuppositions and other "mental-models," especially with duty-bound law-enforcement personnel. Even your personal "language-skills" can enhance or limit your citizen-interaction. Your field-of-attention skills encouraged your interaction with a citizen whose interaction-skills are framed by their personal prejudices and presuppositions. Without quality citizen-interaction, the essence of police-sciences will never be realized. Scientist Timothy Ferris reminds us that science, especially police-sciences, "rests on a tripod whose legs are *hypothesis, observation, and faith.*" Like Albert Einstein, law-enforcement must also ignore, disregard or transform "noise" into viable and helpful "signals" that lead to meaningful and quality citizen-interaction ("objectively-reliable-data.") Like the physicist, a police-officer's "theory" about what was just observed in the community (limited reference frame), will not be proven true by one observation, but by additional future multiple observations and verifications. Was your theory based on an automatic and arbitrarily determined cause and effect "frame-of-mind," your default position and mode of operation? Is your default position correct and pertinent for the situation you responded to?

COGNITIVE DISSONANCE

BEHAVIORAL INTERPRETATION

The "reality" of the phenomenon and meaning of "consciousness," as Nobel physicist Eugene Wigner explained, "does not have the same meaning for all of us." Benjamin Libet reminds us of the *"illusion of conscious control."* When you "think" you have consciously decreed to pull the trigger of your firearm; your mind does have the veto power to interrupt the impulse. Timothy Ferris called this process about your mind's veto power, a "flattering illusion that controls the game." Your mind is merely playing "catch-up" after the original impulse to fire your weapon. You may rationalize why you fired your weapon as you thought the secondary thought, "do not fire," while ignorant of the real reason you fired your weapon. Your personal thought-integration-processes will automatically explain, justify and account for your behavioral interpretation, even fabricated "truthiness," including cognitive dissonance. How "free" is your "free-will?" Does the "feeling-of-effort," guarantee free-will-success; or is it simply unconscious conditioned "responses" empowered only as "possibilities-not-certainties"?

"Perhaps our unconscious self is our real self. The conscious self we believe we know so well, interact, and mingle with 'others' is merely a mask, a disguise, or a cloaking-device we use until we are the last person to die in our lifetime. Humans have automatic-emotional responses. These can also be learned—and it is possible to unlearn them if they are counter-productive or unhelpful." From POLICING PRIVATE PERSONALITIES

LEARNED CONTEXT EXPECTATIONS

Michael Gazzaniga explains that most of our behavior is not really controlled by conscious thought processes. We predominately utilize automatic subconscious processes—all out of our awareness. Humans do not think-out behaviorally, every step and interaction movement. What have you intentionally programmed, or allowed to be programmed into your premotor cortex. <u>Are your own aggressive tendencies, holding you hostage</u>? Most of the choices you make in life, are unconscious choices. Law-enforcement requires constant "first-impression" analysis bathed in hidden variables that automatically activates unconscious context, categorical judgments and pre-programmed motor-programming. When dealing with victims, witnesses and suspects—especially in life-or-death emergency situations; mental information/image flow from your cerebral cortex to your "striatum," is processed. The striatum, **utilizing learned expectations** based on past interactive behavioral responses; develops pertinent and useful information that is integrated as "<u>learned-context</u>," for immediate and automatic use. The striatum's learned-context is not just for instantaneous behavior modification. This learned-context assists with preparatory movement activity and self-initiated movements—beyond your present moment concerns. This helps ensure your mentally and physically prepared for future events, "intention-to-outcome." Goal-directed behavior utilizing "reward/punishment" related striatal activity, still requires dopamine-neurons to determine your emotional interpretation and subsequent "feeling" physical response. This affects and infects all your future behavior out of your awareness; you will not recognize the past situation's negative influence on here/now behavior.

"Police-Citizen Interaction—sometimes we feed off each other or catch (<u>contagious emotional feedback</u>) each other's emotional behavior; usually not the good or helpful de-escalation emotional expression. Your perceptual systems are always (consciously and unconsciously) interpreting the 'status of the environment.' All law-enforcement has to do when we respond to complex emotional situations, is to evaluate and determine emotional-meaning and <u>predict future behaviors immediately</u> concerning people we have probably never met before!" From POLICING PRIVATE PERSONALITIES, Sam Luckey

DOPAMINE-NEURON SATISFACTION

Unexpected rewards get the attention of your dopamine-neurons. When your expectation related activity detects behavioral significance involving an unexpected multiple reward; dopamine influenced adaptive-learning, as a reinforcer, appropriate or inappropriate, develop. What is considered "rewarding" to someone in law-enforcement is as diverse as the dispatches we respond to. This dopamine reinforcement may influence your personal "reward-dependent" unconscious behavior selection processing; "rewards" that are not healthy, safe, wise or beneficial for community and self! How functional are your "executive" mental discipline and control processes in recognizing "deviation" and "error-codes," when trying to console your dopamine-neurons? Bad habits and addictions may develop when forces out-of-your awareness, internal and external, try to entertain and satisfy your dopamine-neurons. Neurochemical differentiation is difficult to recognize its influence on your thought processes. Especially when trying to determine if it is appropriate for you and community, during time-sensitive emergency dispatches that influence your neuropeptide expression, and subsequent influence on long-term dopamine-neuron modification input. Your future information-processing happiness determining self is influenced here/now thru past behavior as experience—dopamine projecting itself into your personality of the moment—every moment as judgments and expectations!

"Neurobiologist Candace Pert taught that 'your mind is in every cell of your body.' That is how your mind can not only physiologically control your body, but it can also 'override genetic programming.' What we call 'direct personal experience' has been hijacked by our own mental processes. Our perceptual system has evolved where anticipation (especially automatic emergency behavior) allows perception alone to activate the body and prepare it chemically

(physiologically) for any emergency contingency. Even before you cognitively become aware of a 'problem.'"

DOPAMINE-NEURON

DOMINATED PLEASURE-SEEKING

For law-enforcement, your neuron response "magnitude" recognition of **primary-rewards** may be a potent distraction, leading you to miss other reward predictors in your field-of-vision. Transmission of nerve-impulses is a two-way dopamine influenced dance; afferent and efferent utilization of your central nervous system. Do you trust this undisciplined out-of-your awareness, indiscriminate dopamine dictated pleasure-reward search, especially where excitatory afferents along with hyperpolarized and depolarized neurons, send your mind? We all have naturally occurring feedback regulation of neurotransmitter release concerning dopaminergic and glutamatergic signals to striatal neurons, involving both postsynaptic and presynaptic interactions. We are well-designed to determine interoceptive mental thought disturbances that must first, unfortunately, break through your dopamine-neuron dominated pleasure seeking undisciplined inner-turmoil. You may be excellent at "**pattern-recognition**," but dopamine influences which outside-stimuli detected "context," needs, wants, and desires, are registered into working memory, especially police-memory association-recognition. Dopamine influences your ability to plan and coordinate complex behaviors, especially the "strength" of your convictions about your abilities. Your motor-control outputs can become more mentally distracted hesitant, if your dopamine-neuron reinforcements are engrossed by **rewards not present**—classical conditioned police behavioral response.

"For most of us, 'thinking has become a disease.' Reinvent yourself, beginning with here/now thought processes. Take charge of your internal dialogue—it is harder than you imagined. Thinking about

previous thoughts is really just another thought. Thinking about your own thoughts as a disciplined or undisciplined form of self-awareness. Recognize when 'self-importance' becomes the primary factor directing your behavioral interaction with 'others'" From POLICING PRIVATE PERSONALITIES, SAM LUCKEY

Positive reinforcement learning mechanisms, require the contribution of striatal dopamine processes as mediators of reinforcement, considered positive reinforcement command signals. We become experts at determining outside-stimuli that predict positive reinforcement. The question is, do you have any behavioral-control over awareness and attention when your dopamine-neurons are in need of some kind of emotional-fix; further influencing negatively, your memory storage, expectation, interpretation, and synaptic efficacy. Is this the long-term kind of heterosynaptic long-lasting enhancement you desire? Remember that Parkinsons is considered a "disease of the dopamine system;" the symptoms of which normally do not appear until most of your dopamine-neurons have died off. Medical dopamine agonists work so well in some patients, that they develop abnormal (for them) behaviors, like addictions to gambling. Drop the dopamine agonists, the tremors return but gambling and other abnormal behaviors usually stop.

STIMULUS REWARD POLICING

Dopamine neurons have been evolutionarily designed and primed to be your "**predictor,**" especially when determining what preceded the outside-stimuli patterns that lead to your interpretation of "reward." Unpredictable rewards can activate your dopamine neurons almost four times more than a predictable reward, possibly making you "**stimulus-dependent.**" Consider this dopamine-surge as urgent and immediate communication to your executive self-control center; something unusual or novel has been detected, outside stimuli needs your attention-intensity. Dopamine-neurons get obsessed when "patterns" are hinted that cannot be deciphered, fictive error learning. Optimistic possibility rules, random processes be damned, the *"gamblers-fallacy"* or simple *"loss-aversion."* Past rewards need to be impulsively duplicated as your *"primitive reward circuits"* have needs! Behavior based on your emotional instincts as a "reference-point," can be "felt" or assumed to be reliable, if you never verify accuracy or admit when you were steered wrong. Dopamine neurons may be why you are spending your retirement money on high-interest credit card debt—impulsivity needs some kind of resistance. Rational planning, especially if it involves long-term benefits, not immediate benefits; utilizes a different area of your brain, than when you impulsively believe you NEED something right now! All you have to do is learn how to bypass your emotional brain. Automatic emotional responses can save your life, they can also narrow your perception of outside-stimuli. Auto-responses can buy you a few seconds before thinking processes finally kick-in.

FINDDING PATTERNS AND ORIGINAL SOLUTIONS

OCD (*obsessive-compulsive-disorder*) is usually associated with uncontrolled urges to clean and count objects, or verify devices are off and doors are really-really locked, this time. In all my classes that discussed OCD; I never remember any indicators that a police-officer, may have OCD-like tendencies when it comes to routine-patrol—constant exposure to violence and response prevention treatment—or, we may get "sick." Police-citizen interaction requires both "deliberate-thought," alongside minor automated unconscious mental processes. Sometimes a police-officer is triggered immediately to initiate behavior based on "first-impressions," that may or may not be appropriate. Your prefrontal cortex will usually save-the-day, and enlighten you that this first-impression was wrong—with the mental processing capability to analyze your citizen-interaction from multiple angles. Abstract thought skills may prove pertinent when surprising creative associations arise that seem more plausible, especially when your initial impression fails to assist citizen or officer. Admitting failure and changing strategies may be hard for OCD leaning police-officers. Your prefrontal-cortex is how you understand or realize the **"act-of-recognition."** Your experience, professional and personal, influenced your emotional-library which further influences your skills at finding patterns, original solutions, determine relevance and other task prioritizations. Fortunately, humans have the ability to maintain in their mind for an additional, few seconds, outside stimulus that needs further mental analysis, considered the *"restructuring phase"* in problem solving. Your "new idea" may be built on previous and current thoughts.

"Recognize the differences between 'impulsive-desires' and 'intuitive-knowing.' There is intentionality behind consciousness. Being 'aware that you are aware' is a different mental process than simple awareness. Our 'objective' version of reality—is really subjective interpretation. From POLICING PRIVATE PERSONALITIES, SAM LUCKEY

EXPECTATIONS AND FALSE ASSUMPTIONS

Describe your personal *"essence of rationality."* There are times when a police-trainer finds appropriate moments to teach a rookie that it is possible to, *"think-to-much."* Your own thought processes can incapacitate you, or even, get you distracted or killed. Sometimes citizens or other police-officers introduce variables into your investigation, that are not associated. You have to determine which "facts" are here/now important for your investigation. Sometimes, more information impedes goal-directed activity and clarity. Unintended extra-self-conscious behavior can make you **"present-without-presence."** Emotional-wisdom is real, and can help assess your actual preferences as felt-feelings. Preference explanation can be difficult, while "feeling" right naturally occurs; like the placebo effect as expected experience (prefrontal cortex modulation). Expectations impact your behavior. **False-assumptions** misinterpreted as rational-expectations, may also create reality-distortion inappropriate for law-enforcement responsibilities and obligations. False expectations become false assumptions—experience modulation—defects in our community need our attention, whether the community wants it or not. Have someone point to an object in your field-of-vision, and unless you consciously intend it, you will glance or focus on the object, especially "annoying" images. The anchoring effect of this object on you will further impact immediate and future decision-making. Even a random non-related number, will illogically infect your future **decision making**. I used to believe that "unnecessary information" just had to be ignored. Clinical investigation into your reasoning skills/processes, revealed that unnecessary information, especially planted or disguised information, will infect your later decision-making skills.

"Your 'self-expression' begins as an 'act-of-thought,' a unified process, not two separate events. We can still gain and experience knowledge about outside-stimuli without the use of language but it is a hard habit to overcome." "Immediate and direct experience can be overpowered by a simple unchallenged negative thought, especially self-energized social-signals and other unintended non-verbal communication." From POLICING PRIVATE PERSONALITIES, SAM LUCKEY

INTERFERENCE THOUGHT PATTERNS

As amazing as your prefrontal cortex is, experts report that just **seven pieces** of information data, can overwhelm the average human, even increase the likelihood you will choose an unhealthy lifestyle and make other poor decisions. **Impulse control** is made harder when your prefrontal cortex is challenged. The textbook description used dietary issues of impulse control. It seems to me that police-work impulse control is vulnerable to these seven pieces of info-limit. We are running, with a gun in one hand, a radio-mic in the other, shouting orders, hearing orders, hearing radio traffic, suspect focus, citizen safety—which is already more than seven-issues we face at the same time. Clinical investigations have clearly revealed that **more deliberation** does not always mean better decision-making. Everybody operates more from unconscious behavioral processes, until your prefrontal cortex monitor introduces interference thought patterns like second-guessing performance anxiety. Being a police-officer at a complicated emotional violent incident, feels like you are on a stage while citizen-audience distracts and monitors you. The *"descriptive-adjectives"* you use in public, alongside hidden personal mentalese describing the incident or participants, actually influences your physical behavior and mental expectations and ultimately successful de-escalation. Practice the difficult art of thinking more pleasantly, when interacting with certain citizens that may not deserve more respect and effort. Many times, we end our citizen-interaction with a "sounds-good" signal, void of verification feedback intent. The positivity of which may not really be beneficial, but time-constraints prevent us from spending more time and effort in community problem-solving.

"Does your mind (internal-dialogue) or personal disposition prevent 'response-flexibility' when dealing with other people. We interpret, judge, classify and categorize experience. Unconscious thoughts motivate unconscious social-signals and other unintended non-verbal communication." POLICING PRIVATE PERSONALITIES SAM LUCKEY

EMOTIONAL REGULATION SELF-AWARENESS

I believe we are missing signs of OCD exhibited by police-officers involved in police-citizen interaction. Emotionally charged, signs of citizen-deception, impatience being revealed; this is when a police-officers professional personality is revealed to the world.

Sometimes the citizen is unfocused on everything but the actual incident that required a police response. You have to take control of the conversation and uncover important details—requiring the initiating of calculated **interruption timing sequences**, without upsetting the citizen. Your demeaner, body-language, distance from citizen, hand on your pistol by habit, your facial expression when lied to, level of respect afforded the citizen, and a dozen other personal habits; are also evaluated by the citizen, resulting in on-going behavioral modification—for the better, we hope. Working alongside certain police-officers you observe their personal OCD behavioral modification variations reflected during police-citizen interaction. Passive, but insistent thoughts that distract from the situation you responded to; can get you killed as easily as fear-based thoughts. A detached perspective can be proper at times, distracting at others. Your rational self needs prefrontal cortex "emotional-regulation" self-awareness, not necessarily less emotion. A police-officer may witness a citizen "expressing" impulsive emotions, who is unable to properly "explain" their feelings. Simple cognitive skills can inhibit impulses that distract or prevent you from completing goals and objectives—transcend your impulses.

"Experts remind us that your behavior is 'brain-based.' Your brain exists in space because it is a physical structure, while your mind 'operates in time alone.' Can you proactively consciously reprogram your unconscious? Recognize that 'thoughts" take physical form. Your cells respond to your thoughts while your mind leads your body." From POLICING PRIVATE PERSONALITIES Sam Luckey

I could not find any literature confirming if OCD influences bias and/or prejudice. If your unconsciously convinced and believe in racial-stereotypes (even out of your awareness), your unconscious will convince your conscious processes, so-skillfully and out of your awareness—YOU WILL DENY IT! Racism will raise its ugly influence during your police-citizen interaction. Racist ideology and other "theoretical preconceptions" never exist only at the unconscious level. Racism flavors everything, consciously expressed ambiguous "exposure points," especially during emotionally charged exchanges and incidents—that mandate police-responses. Especially police-specific trained and untrained, ritualistic learned-pre-programmed habitual compulsive behaviors—that you unconsciously empower thru brain-controls-body obligations. Authors and neuroscientists I respect, have (pretty-much) convinced me that there is no such thing as a mind that operates independent of the brain. Brain anomalies cloud the mind. It is my brain that creates "mindful-awareness." Introspection is self-examination brain-activity—that does not involve a separate mental individual or mind. I'll have to keep re-MINDING myself of that—in unity and internally, not as a separate person-brain-or mind—absolute unity, and on-and on-and on. It is just electro-chemical impulses out of my awareness and control—until I am the last person in my lifetime, to die.

BEHAVIOR-USER ILLUSION AND PERSONAL FREEDOM

Is your mental-discomfort more perceived as emotionally-learned feelings of "intense-discomfort," or, "ambiguous" mood-reassurance seeking, desires, needs or wants? What is the driving-force behind your OCD. We now know that there really are internal biological conditions operating powerfully behind your mind's bewilderment. A citizen or police-officer experiencing powerful distress OCD behavioral-urges, is **not seeing reality as it really is**— incompatible electro-chemical impulses, synoptically bouncing brain pathways meant for another time and place. Dangerous for both parties. What we **pay attention to now**, inner and outer unified awareness—creates physical changes in your brain; "structure and future functioning." It took several police-responses, after returning from my first tour in Korea, working as a MP patrolman at Fort Bliss, Texas; for my backup to recognize when my feet/legs would go into a semi-relaxed martial arts preparatory stance, when face-to-face with unruly soldiers. Potentially related to Dr. Jeffrey M. Schwartz paradigm shift interpretation involving "personal-freedom-behavior" filtered through **"user-illusion,"** or, empowered moral-responsibility. After dealing with unruly Korean citizens and American soldiers, who all seemed to have martial-arts training, I began the unconscious habit of preparatory stances that would allow my "kicks" to initially protect me, and gain some distance and advantage. I brought that habit to Texas. This MP and soldier interaction may get interesting. I had not even noticed that I employed such a stance-maneuver **(motor-programs)** during typical police-responses—OCD in nature, or simple old-fashioned ego-dystonic characteristics?

Perhaps, the only reason I did not habitually put my hand on my .45, or feel comforted by the feel of it; was because I had no faith in the weapons age. The slide was so loose, it must have been used at the Battle of the Bulge or other historical events. I had to point out to one MP, that when he approached soldiers—**habitually seeking "their-attention;"** he had a bad-habit (OCD?) of first timidly touching, then grabbing their shirt or jacket (unconscious **control impulses**-to impulsively gain pro-active pre-control advantage over soldier?), before he began speaking, or any real-justification to be making physical-contact. He immediately denied that he did, while other MPs explained that he really did! Then he automatically stated without hesitation, that he was "just being friendly." Most brain-biochemical imbalances seem normal to the experiencer—until behavior indicates something "Abby-normal." Is the statement that we use our mind to know our mind, no longer relevant; if the mind is just another brain-function? Do we go back to, "we use our **brain to know our brain**?" I'm actually fine with either statement. Just for inner-clarity when I think "need to clear my mind," or is it now my brain, or, where do thoughts fit in? Perhaps this is why 99% of law-enforcement and soldiers do not intend or practice daily recognizing just a few non-productive, feed-back loop memory work-driven—thoughts, that do not deserve such reliving and reenergizing over-and-over. Positive thoughts that do not support your negativity-detour (anxiety, anger self-pity?), will be subconsciously re-directed further out of your awareness. Help from inside—never arrives! Every bad thought mental response, even false-premise thoughts, become fact if they are stored in the unconscious that way.

APPROACH/WITHDRAW/APPROACH/WITHDRAWL

EXCITATORY/INHIBITORY/EXCITATORY/INHIBITORY

What are your specialized personal and most community-positive adaptive behaviors—requiring sacrifice and behavioral-modification for the sake of your community? Does your police "on-duty" list match your "off-duty pro-social" list? Which self/other us/them adaptive behaviors did you assign only one category, and why? Start with one bad thought; if you have so many bad-thought false-messages, that you can't seem to choose just a few! "Mind-over-matter," or: Brain-matter-over all other matter. Your brain-power, trained-or-untrained, over your body and everything "other" in your universe." Brains—really do matter. Brain-matter producing "mind-as-by-product," which affects and infects the original brain-matter, which originally produced the "mind-as-by-product." Approach-withdrawal or excitatory-inhibitory. We all have feed-forward and feed-backward neuronal processes that seize control of our attention-skills—taking us out of the present moment—not good for law-enforcement. Psychiatry researcher Jeffrey Schwartz questions the validity of denying the existence of a "mind," which conveniently eliminates any questions of researching the mind/body problem. Your nervous system as a "action-potential" communication system, monitors your environment and outside-stimuli in vigilant-awareness, ready to release packets of chemical neurotransmitters, **extracellular signal molecules**, for your internal consumption. Are you in full-control of your "signal" molecules? A police-officer's visual behavior requires complicated subcortical

32

retina-to-brain pathways in order for you to initiate the appropriate signaling molecules.

RATIONALITY BECAME A LIABILITY

Are you able to physiologically self-analyze causes of your neuron over-stimulation and subsequent behavioral auto-responses? Improper or excess hormone or endocrine agents will increase the likelihood that your emotional library of learned responses, will dose you repeatedly, in a feedback-loop, improper for the situation you find yourself in. A police-officer can be overwhelmed with so-much incoming information, that it **disrupts prefrontal-cortex** mental analysis and obstructs understanding. Even long-held moral beliefs and choices can be influenced negatively. We may no-longer internalize the "feelings-of-others." The irrational "madman" that you alone are facing, should be approached as if he still has fully functional reasoning processes. A citizen or police-officer can easily identify "reasons" for poor choices and behavior. Behavior that your emotional brain generates, may require your rational brain to explain it to yourself and others. We will recite never ending "reasons" upon "reasons," for our behavior, as each reason is proved wrong—as we are social-primates primed with impersonal reflexes. Rationality can become a liability. Your prefrontal cortex may become a "reason" information filter to the world. Cognitive dissonance is easy to hide from the world—selective interpretation. What is recognized, may not be present or not related to your dispatch.

"Your perception and interpretation of the situation, real or imagined, has more influence on your actions in the here and now than the actual reality of what is happening right in front of you. You are running around like a pre-programmed social-robot, totally unaware of what you have been instructed and pre-programmed (role) to portray, believe and, ultimately who exactly programmed you---PISS POOR PRIOR PRE-PROGRAMMING! Are you introducing

action-behavior that hinders or conflicts with attaining positive de-escalation results?" From POLICING PRIVATE PERSONALITIES, Sam Luckey

REALITY-BASED COGNITIVE STRATEGIES

A police-officer's decision-making processing should be statistically better than random chance. The dopamine system internalizes all your experience, the good and the bad. I spent over a decade working with autistic-children who had a poorly developed fusiform-face area, making it hard to focus or recognize the important non-verbal behavior, faces provide. They were excellent at object recognition, as some experts believe that instead of using the fusiform face area for facial recognition skills, they use brain processes meant for objects. Autism has been called a "permanent form of **mind blindness**" and "the most inheritable of all neurologic conditions" by author Jonah Lehrer. A police-officer relies on prefrontal-cortex processing. Some citizens easily and conveniently, cultivate and justify behavioral ignorance, empowering their belief that they can talk their way out of the situation. Law enforcement may be detecting patterns that are just coincidences and act improperly. We may assign **causation onto a citizen,** when it was simple **correlation**. We have an addiction to information that is not always positive, sometimes actually constricting healthy thinking processes. Your cognitive strategies should be determined and influenced by the actual situation.

"Our internal habits and proficiency at 'making-judgments' from our biased experience of personal reality, contradicting actual 'reality,' directs what little 'attention' skills we have towards petty, vindictive self-grandiose interactions. Experts remind us that your behavior is 'brain-based.' Your brain exists in space because it is a physical structure, while your mind 'operates in time alone.' Can you proactively consciously reprogram your unconscious? Recognize that 'thoughts' take physical form. Your cells respond to your

thoughts while your mind leads your body. Where does your mind take you when you are off-duty and seeking peace-of-mind? Are you a hostage to your own mind?" POLICING PRIVATE PERSONALITIES, Sam Luckey

EMOTIONAL MEMORY AND MODULATION

Police-officers interact with impulsive and insensitive citizens who live a life of "social-isolation;" which has programmed them to no longer care or even consider the emotional status or feelings of yourself and other citizens. Every situation is different and requires specific cognitive strategies for every situation. This is a good habit to develop and expand your understanding. Are you aware and calm enough to detect when emotional or violent incidents are negatively exceeding your mature and professional **self-control limitation** "personal-threshold" emotional modulation, and subsequently generating action-potentials you may not be proud of. You are no longer a Peace-Officer. During dangerous situations police routinely respond to, our sensory neurons utilizing chemical synapses, will not send more powerful action-potentials to get our attention; the "threshold" needed has already been established. Instead, the outside stimulus causes our action potentials to simply generate more frequently, (not more powerfully), as a signal-priority. Your physiological response to the chemical nature of hormones, are not always immediate. Hormonal biological actions target specific cells utilizing signal-transduction and subsequent gene transcription alteration. Fast-acting catecholamine hormones and peptides attaching to plasma-membrane receptors, causing second-messenger cascades. Slower-acting hormones like steroids, that target specific cell-groups, influence the various proteins the cell synthesizes by altering the cell nucleus transcription of proteins. **Internal biological feedback** mechanisms are required to keep hormones in-line, regulated and effective. You were probably never trained in "autorhythmicity," but, if you were not an expert at naturally and unconsciously triggering your own heart's

35

contractions, you would not be reading this. Nerve impulses to your heart are supplied by the parasympathetic and the sympathetic nervous system. A well-meaning police-officer stopping a vehicle that just sped past a school bus with the "stop-arm" activated and extended; citing statistical evidence of why this driver's action was bad, should be aware that statistical evidence does not excite our moral emotions. A police-officer would have more effectiveness with personal stories about **vehicle-pedestrian accidents**—instead of statistics. If the citizen still does not seem attentive, I used photographs which I kept in my briefcase.

<u>LOGICAL REASONS FOR HIDDEN-BIAS</u>

Matter generates mind. We also have "dark-matter," a misnomer that does not describe what is intended. Try looking for videos describing "matter-less matter" and immaterial-realms. When you intend or think your material-body to refrain an "act," that may be considered a "committed-act." Especially when dealing with an emotionally challenging violent citizen that we have allowed to trigger our **"justified"** crossed an ambiguous imaginary line. We catch ourself about to commit illegal in-the-street justice, and in a "committed-act," we stay professional. When it happens; remember your introspective-recognition of doing what was right. It will make identifying the next time you're about to cross-the-line, easier and timelier—every time you do what is right. Experts remind us that thoughts as **"internal-disagreements"** and competing thoughts, are not unhealthy when you are making decisions. Some decisions seem "logical," while others seem decided from your emotional unconscious level—which creates social-decision "feelings," your dopamine reward pathways or uncertainty. <u>Self-delusion is easier to initiate than actually recognizing it.</u> Even simple shopping-desire decisions are emotionally flavored—primed pleasure centers. Your insula keeps your spending habits pertinent and under budget, which stores create displays and signage that satisfies your insula out-of-your awareness. Credit cards bypass your insula because you do not really feel any pain or less money in your wallet—dangerous for the weak minded. The immaterial-mind exerts control over our physical body? Your immaterial-mind possesses **"hidden-biases,"** that do not just "guide-your-behavior." These hidden-biases guide your behavior out of your awareness so easily and masterfully; you will deny bias-exhibition that you just expressed, was unintended. You will out-of-your awareness, immediately verbalize a "logical-reason" without evaluation, justifying why you said or did what you did. Reasons that just seem logical or reasonable, if they also happen to back-up your unconscious belief-systems; will be intuited as truthful and correct—beyond second-guessing mental conflicts. Even a police-officers social-group-interaction is pre-programmed culturally as indoctrination; powerfully and self-righteously, intruding into your unconscious thought processes.

HABITS OF THOUGHT/AUTOMATIC ASSOCIATION

Insignificant mental content that you hold out of your awareness, guides your attentional behavior, verbal, visual and physical movement. Insignificant mental content that is inaccessible to introspection, still functions as **"unconscious inference"** and all the interference subsequently created. No matter how clear your visual-field is, visual-information still requires a "mind" to interpret—usually based on "habits-of-thought" that you usually do not know you carry or empower. It is disappointing that my psychology college classes back in the old-days, did not, or, perhaps "censored" from my textbooks, any mention of **"unconscious cognition"** or "implicit cognition." Behaviorists seemed to control all the key positions at schools back then. If you also were "schooled" in the old-days, just start with internet videos on those two subjects. Then consider going back to school for some updates. On-duty, or off-duty, police are **"automatic association-making machines."** How accurate are you involving self-recognizing memory-errors and false recollections. Humans ended up

37

evolutionarily designed to humorously defend false recollections if challenged, more than true recollections. How easily are your memories retroactively altered by other police-officers, citizens, self-awareness or stress? Just because your undisciplined thought processes frequently allow improper or self-defeating thoughts the status of "conscious-awareness;" this frequency-rate does not equate or validate into the real-world. The actual world not trapped in your mind!

Negative thoughts left unchallenged can become social-meaning **"anchoring-points"** from which you interpret and filter the entire universe. Vivid negative thoughts are not valid, just because they are vivid in memory recall ease and self-awareness. Our emotional programming concerning interactive social-choices, originally neuronally designed and tested in our ancestor's primitive environment; still influence our automatic social skills, especially our library of personal habitual emotional displays. How many "unrecognized-untruths" have you uttered today? Police-officers have an unusual occupation that requires routinely, without expressing hostility, to say well-intended "untruths," to avoid hurting a citizen's emotional self-awareness, in an effort at de-escalation. Honestly, sometimes these well-intended "untruths" we express are meant to avoid our own feelings. We also have thoughts that we censor or block "self-talk" to ourselves about. Self-righteous self-deception.

"Do you describe your 'sense-of-self' as a basic simple to understand 'core-self;' or do you recognize your 'sense-of-self' as a multitude of differing 'social-selves?' How much of your personality is socially dictated, socially described, socially programmed, socially prescribed, culturally and socially determined? Whichever social-self is needed, is the one that bubbles up on auto-pilot as your personality-of-the-moment—determining and influencing the 'capacity to produce behavior' and the just as important 'impulses for action.' Are you content with allowing random auto-pilot

personalities controlling your interpersonal social interaction?"
POLICING PRIVATE PERSONALITIES SAM LUCKEY

NEUROTRANSMITTER AUTO-POLICE BEHAVIOR

When you are involved with complicated police-citizen interaction, and the citizen screams from built-up primal behavioral stress, "Nothing-#%&@-matters!' You pay attention because that statement **"really-#&&@-matters**!" Matter is considered by contemporary physicists to be—a "concentrated form of energy." Illusion involving multiple mind-processes, basically just the effect of brain-matter—your "reality." Can you identify personal conscious processes that are not routine neural processes and neurochemical reactions? Have you mastered the release of neurotransmitters (type, strength, duration and just as important—remove all traces of the neurotransmitter in preparation for the next one), for optimal-police-citizen-interaction-behavior? You have a personal neuronal-based image-library of reliably predictable policing **pre-programmed** emergent mental-processes at your beckoning? OR—your action and mental-behavioral responses at complicated dispatches merely rely on whatever auto-police-behavior bubbles up in-the-moment, based merely on "trust" that it will work out best for citizen, community and officer?

"Self-deception is initiated or carried out by whom? Self-deception is recognized and realized by whom? Self-deception is cured or healed by whom? Self-deception is avoided and prevented by whom? Seems like an awful lot of 'single-self' 'single-selves!' Recognizing self-deception is judgment determined by whom? Who is making judgment? Who was deceived? Who is being judged? Could you know about another 'you' or 'self-state' if the other 'self-state' did not want you to know? Can one 'self-state' be more powerful than all the other 'self-states?' Could this be another reason why you wake up feeling so tired? Are you sure that one of your 'self-states' is not borrowing your body during the night? Could that be the

reason you have realized you have just shot another person and do not remember pulling the trigger? Is it possible that all these 'self-states' that you carry can become 'group-behavior?' Did you swear your oath as an 'individual' in a group, or as a mental 'group' into a much-larger group? From POLICING PRIVATE PERSONALITIES SAM LUCKEY

Going to High School in Gary Indiana, and working full-time in the evening required constant vigilance of your surroundings at work, and while walking anywhere! At that time in the early 1970s, Gary was fighting Detroit and Washington D.C. for the horrible title of "murder-capital of the USA." Are life-threatening situational awareness skills, regular-citizen or law-enforcement, consistent with what a neuroscientist would consider OCD? A "behaviorist" maybe? Our War in Vietnam had recently ended, and budget cuts left us MP patrol-cars with 100,000-to-200,000-mile odometer readings, since we used staff-car rejects. One patrol-car would die, if you made the mistake of using your overheads while your headlights were on. I remember OCD type behavior, with particular MPs rejecting and choosing their patrol car for the night—magical insight, from our limited choice end-of-life military vehicles. I also remember patrolling in the old WWII style Jeeps in Korea, (no hard-top only canvas, no seat-belt, just a thin strap as a door to keep you in.) In Europe, we rented West German civilian vans and cars. As a CID agent in Frankfurt West Germany, I drove a Jetta. During the energy crisis of the 70's, one MP patrol-area at Fort Bliss, was switched to a 3-wheel scooter.

EMOTIONAL BEHAVIOR AND OVERCOMPESATION

Physicist Max Born stressed that "Living matter and clarity are opposites." Author Jonah Lehrer describes that "the default state of the brain is indecisive disagreement." Certainty bathed in self-doubt, conflicting reactions, inner contradictions and the fear of being wrong, is not certainty. Citizen-interaction is rarely clearly defined and productive, until you intend to make it so! Your intelligence involving citizen/community interaction can be improved by focusing on your perception and memory associational skills. Relying more on **positive communication skills** in order to solve this current situation and respond to the next situation seeking a solution. The smoother you solve this situation; means you will carry less emotional baggage into your next dispatch with less overcompensating behaviors. There are good and bad aspects for the police-officer behaving with a *"bias-for-certainty."* Filter your "certainty" with "inner dissonance," assumption verification and examine all information that you find inconvenient or a nuisance—you owe it to your community. Certainty may be an innate tendency, but it is never guaranteed to be true, correct and effective. Do not view competing viewpoints or dissent as an attack on your belief systems or law-enforcement. It would be nice if we only had to focus on important variables concerning an emotional incident, at least narrow down some uncertainty we have; but we will be bombarded with biased and intentionally disguised variables—some important, some merely distractions. Rational thought usually works, unless over-thinking traps your mind in indecision and lack of clarity. Some emergency response decisions can actually be made more correctly utilizing your emotional brain—feeling body and intuitive hunches.

"Automatic categorizations (judgements and assumptions) occur more often when 'stimulus characteristics' do not actually reach or penetrate into conscious awareness. We have been evolutionarily designed to experience 'recognition' before 'recall.' Humans also have the ability to determine 'form-from-motion.' This helps us determine if the movement we think we are observing, could be a human-in-motion." From POLICING PRIVATE PERSONALITIES, Sam Luckey.

SELF-ENHANCED MENTAL FLEXIBILITY

Your unconscious was evolutionarily designed to be more powerfully able to assimilate environmental variability, than your conscious-aware self. Unconscious choices in decision making are revealed as **"feelings;"** which counter-intuitively, highlights the benefit of your being capable for **"rational-analysis,"** alongside **"irrational-emotions."** Experts have proven that your prefrontal-cortex can be "confused" when processing multiple variables (seven variables seems to be average before we become confused or indecisive.) Clinical investigations allow the scientist to actually detect when a subject is making decisions based from the unconscious brain. Subjects were forced to make "emotionally" based decisions, and examine their "feelings" for positivity of the decision, over rational analysis. The emotionally based decisions utilizing "feelings" were clearly more correct for the situation. We incorrectly "assume" that your subconscious mind cannot be skillfully and mindfully self-enhanced; mental-flexibility, through intending skill-development, specifically for mental processes operating out of your awareness. Considering alternate scenarios and possibilities, if time permits, is not a sign of weakness, or indecision. Over-confidence in your "certainty" involving a decision, may lead to ignoring discrepancies and misinterpret evidence as it is presented to you. One particular experiment summarized the results as: "Irrational choosers were the best decision-makers by far." More surprising to me, was the finding that analyzing options longer, resulted in decision-makings that was "less satisfied." You may believe you know your preferences, but analysis usually reveals contradictions involving intent, desire and outcome.

"Selective attention (a property of your mind—your brain's response), modifies your visual-cortex. Our perception processes function better when we are active participants instead of patrolling pre-programmed, bored, annoyed, and passively distracted. The evidence of your senses can be overruled by alternate sensory processing, and a pre-programmed expectation driven mind.

Humans are wired to speed-up our perception processes using 'preconceived-images,' that may not match the reality of your situation." From POLICING PRIVATE PERSONALITIES, Sam Luckey

UNCONSCIOUS COMPETETING BEHAVIORAL OPTIONS

Sometimes, preferential options are so numerous, conscious reflection is not possible for your situation. Humans still possess a few **emotional circuits** from our ancient primitive past, that are not applicable or helpful for modern life, especially policing skills. Even though I have read a dozen books clearly stating that "emotional" choices are best for everyday decision-making that have some emotional flavor, my conscious self is still hesitant to accept the truth of a hundred clinical experiments. Simple unimportant decisions just do not activate emotional analysis/behavior. "Novel" situations may require the influence of reason, in addition to emotional background feelings. Poker players reportedly play worse by ignoring their emotional-feelings during the game. Sometimes your emotions can become overwhelming, requiring intended rational analysis, or the *"reins of cognition"* as experts put it. Your behavior and experience are developed and acted upon, more from unconscious processes and mechanisms, than conscious "willed" behavior. Dr. **John Baugh** calls these unconscious mechanisms, "invisible **patterns in our mind**." Everybody has multiple competing mental processes making it harder to determine which "mental-process" provides the best behavioral option for the situation you were dispatched to. He further describes that when asked, the untrained cannot identify specific instances where our unconscious "influenced our behavior."

"Thoughts, words, objects, things, stimuli and situations can trigger an emotional outburst. What 'triggering-mechanisms' of yours are activated by 'others,' automatically creating 'fixed behavior patterns' that you are not proud of. Do your mental processes routinely make situations better or worse? Can you consciously

prevent your emotional state from influencing your feeling state negatively. Anticipation and prediction, awareness of intention—self and other, are heavily influenced more based on prior experience— than the actual situation you responded to. From POLICING PRIVATE PERSONALITIES, Sam Luckey

LEARNING FROM MISTAKES

BEGINS WITH AN ADMISSION

What a police-officers thinks, knows and understands about a situation dispatched to, includes what you know, and just as importantly, what you do not know! Your analysis of the situation must include <u>what you do not know</u>—the **benefit of experience** and what you do with that experience. Are you as a police-officer too important to be a "student-of-your-errors," and learn-from them? Learning from your mistakes is preparing your brain for future encounters that may not provide time for rehearsal or delayed responses. If time-issues allow it, diversity of viewpoints can help and hinder. Speaking as a group, seems to include behavior that is more "jumping on the bandwagon," than actually dissecting and verify the intentions and goals of the group—allowing some of law-enforcements worse historical events to be condoned, encouraged and covered-up. Humans automatically empower repressing any interoceptive or exteroceptive "signs" that we are mentally unwell or divided; even though we just physically or mentally appeared to ourselves or others as broken. Unconscious awareness is a different mental process than intending to become more aware of unconscious influence on your behavior. It is easy to understand that our experiences in life (past-present and future concerns) influence our behavior. Dr. Baugh describes that we also have a "hidden—past, present, future," that influences our behavior out of our awareness; our unconscious memories, expectations, needs and wants—**goal-directed behavior**.

"A police-officer has to recognize the differences between the 'meaning-of-things,' and the subjective meaning we compulsively and cognitively attach—reality veiled by our interpretation, bias and beliefs. We patrol in 'sensory-awareness' of only about 5% of our patrol-environment. Your senses incoming information and other perceptual activity as "neuron-synaptic patterns;" develop a sensory description image of the world that can only be perceived and analyzed by the way your senses have neuronally evolved, designed and programmed to process and define reality. A limited personal reality, not as reality really is. I call this 'neuronal-simulation-stimulation!'"

PRISONER OF YOUR MIND

Is your **"past,"** really in the past? The influence of your past, meddling in present-tense, infecting routine patrol. For the neuroscientist, the fact that the conscious and unconscious utilize the same brain regions, is intriguing. When police-officers respond to an emotional incident, we are modifying our public and internal behavior and presentation, from an unconscious and consciously "willed" viewpoint. Citizens and other police-officers routinely suggest and influence our behavior from conscious and unconscious motivations. Yours and their **"long-term past" and "short-term past"** influence your reasoning skills for the particular situation you responded to—especially snap-judgments. These effects usually remain hidden from conscious analysis. Which is closer to the "real-you?" Your unconscious self or conscious self? Are you proud of both or blissfully ignorant? Psychologist Philip Tetlock warns that police-officers trying to justify their behavior, may really be just **"prisoners of their preconceptions."** "Associative-learning," an important human skill, seems to have linked our "thoughts" and "emotions" together, especially "emotional display." Some of us are experts at emotional-display. Real or faked emotional display.

45

"Most of us do not really use our mind, our mind uses us! Your mind as an adaptive instrument of survival—is now in charge. Will your mind give you permission to consider this possibility? We need to use our mind to reprogram our mind when our mind leads our mind astray. Is your mind's point-of-view the same view you present to others, civilians and law-enforcement? Does your brain serve your mind? Is this what you intended? From POLICING PRIVATE PERSONALITIES, Sam Luckey

HABITUAL THINKING OR UNCERTAINTY

Neural-plasticity begins with your current thought processes— negative or positive, pro-social or anti-social, respectful of citizen-interaction opportunity or not doing your job! First you have to recognize a specific purpose with goals and objectives concerning an area of your life that you are not proud of. As Dr. Joseph Murphy points out in his book, "The Power of Your Subconscious Mind;" your subconscious mind only knows how to function based on the "laws of belief" that you unconsciously empower, intend and energize. Do you believe everything your mind brings to conscious awareness? Your **beliefs overruling reality**? Does your objective mind and your subjective mind work as a team, or are they not even aware of each other and their differences? Which mind performs "**habitual-thinking**" that is positive and which one performs the negative habitual-thinking? Dr. Mayer asks the reader what their habitual-thinking reaps (cause and effect) for your benefit and/or societies benefit. Your personal "thoughts-feelings-imagery" creates your citizen-interaction successes and failures and subsequently your contentment and happiness in law-enforcement. You can't hide your out-of-control thought processes from your subconscious mind and automatic habitual reactions and responses. A police-officer experiencing a *"twinge-of-uncertainty,"* may only be processing *"**antagonistic-reactions**"* between their worrying *insula* and their all-powerful *prefrontal cortex*. Pretending won't fool your own subconscious, while it may work temporarily on your co-workers.

"Thoughts as 'attitudes of your mind,' limit behavior options, energize and program your associational (context and category) social-interaction with other humans, who are also limited by their personal 'attitudes of their mind,' in another social-neural feedback loop needing policing and policies." From POLICING PRIVATE PERSONALITIES, Sam Luckey

Clinical investigation has proven that when your insula and prefrontal cortex conflict, humans will occasionally "trick-themselves" into ending their internal debate, and choose any solution, even if that solution is "dead-wrong!" Intending "reason" does not mean we cannot use reason to justify illogical conclusions and summarizations—self-delusion. Selective interpretation and biased-memory may turn your prefrontal-cortex into a negatively "biased-information-filter." Privately, "**certainty imposes consensus**," whether factual or not—author Jonah Lehrer. Faulty feelings of "certainty," will never need challenging analysis. Your "self" will be thrilled at never having to admit you were wrong; because you never felt any mental-dissonance potential after-reflection—just another "***prisoner-of-pre-conceptions***" and vague intuitions, in your prized thought processes of superiority. Indecisive disagreement is a thing of the past. You never worry that you were wrong! The faulty bliss of not recognizing your personal habitual "conflicting-reactions" to your environment—differing perspective analysis never enters your mind as a needed option. Effective **unconscious-repression** out-of-your-awareness, never needs to be backed up by intending conscious repression. You won't notice a thing and never recognize that you just secured another unconscious belief into your faulty reasoning processing social-belief system. Repression without the memory of repressing being activated or remembered. Similar to the "plausible-stories" children defend their behavior by telling adults, or, even other children.

"Undisciplined, habitual thoughts are as powerful as the words you speak. Have you mastered 'emotionally motivated thought,' and 'thoughtfully motivated emotion?' Do you 'feel' intuition is an 'external-learning' or a 'internal-knowing.'" From POLICING PRIVATE PERSONALITIES Sam Luckey

ASSUMPTION CONTRADICTIONS

Even a police-officer's search for *"cognitive-closure"* can prematurely end functional desperately needed on-scene analysis productivity. An over-confident police-officer may become *"impervious-to-new-information,"* especially competing viewpoints, no-longer able to tolerate dissent—decision quality = ZERO! Important variables at the crime-scene were disregarded or missed because our preconceptions as expectations, distort cognitive mental processing. Neuroscientists have clinically proven, that even having all the necessary information presented to you; your search for **cognitive-closure certainty**, may negatively eliminate conflicting opposition research—automatically, out-of-your awareness. Your investigation has been solved, and you have no loose-ends to follow up on! Without any assumption-contradictions, you are confidently sure there are no competing hypotheses. The same way that author Jonah Lehrer describes poker players, we can also describe police-officers: Both poker players and law-enforcement develop strategies utilizing, "rational-analysis" and "irrational emotion." Excess crime-scene variables may confuse your prefrontal cortex. Simply ask another police-officer to handle a few of your excess variables during your neuronal simulation situation stimulation! Contemplating alternatives takes so much time.

"Thoughts remodel your brain; energize behavior, and we act as if we do not have the ability to control them. The biggest influence on your next thought is usually the effortless thought that led up to what you are thinking here/now—non-stop! Take charge of your thoughts. Do not ignore the thoughts that indicate trouble. We can learn better ways to 'learn.' We can think better ways to think."
From POLICING PRIVATE PERSONALITIES, Sam Luckey.

OVERWHELMING VARIABLES AND EMOTIONAL INPUT

During your investigation, if you have an epiphany or develop a big-solution, this will obviously alter your investigative plan. Unfortunately, the big solution idea may contaminate your interpretation of existing evidence and yet to be discovered evidence. This happened to me a few times when I was misdirected by a suspect once, and another police-officer who was so sure of himself, that I readily went along with his big solution idea. I was a rookie and it never happened again. A police-officer explaining or deciphering their **reasons as "preferences,"** is also exceedingly more cognitively challenging than you would believe. Once you have established your ambiguous and now established preferences, neuroimaging will prove your **unconscious preference** and belief system is out-of-your control and awareness. You may have simply focused on the wrong variable that may not really be relevant for your investigation—misinterpreting subjective desires and goals. When your prefrontal-cortex is overburdened, even a police-officer under time-constraint issues, may oversimplify the scene, ignoring options without clearly identifying reasons—**preferential misinterpretation.** Experts point-out that minor easy decision-making are the problems that should be consciously analyzed and considered, since your emotional library won't be activated. Clinical investigation declares that complicated decisions involving overwhelming variables, that mute prefrontal-cortex decision-making processes; should be given time to detect emotional-flavoring and feelings we have been conditioned to ignore. That is, *"emotional-input,"* with just enough rational analysis for the severity of the situation.

"We were never really taught how to manipulate our own thoughts—yet seem awfully energized to manipulate the thoughts of 'others.' Recognizing facts at a crime scene is a different mental process than discovering those same facts, or being fed facts, 'transfer-of-learning' by other police-officers." From *POLICING PRIVATE PERSONALITIES,* Sam Luckey

NEVER FINISH A NEGATIVE STATEMENT

One of the more enjoyable aspects of my law-enforcement experience around the world, was facing in the strangest of conditions, situations requiring abstract approaches, NOVEL community social-problems needing a police-response. NOVEL situations still require the influence of reason—especially <u>if you do not know what you do not know</u>. Oddly, what you do not know should be incorporated into planning, goals and objectives! Have you ever summarized the **"laws-of-your-mind"** that you energize, promote and humorously defend, especially viewpoint diversity? While in a position-of-authority, we can easily "justify" expressing irrational emotions "authoritatively." Dr. Mayer has a wonderful quote about negativity, that <u>I wished I had known back in my law-enforcement days</u>: "Never finish a **negative statement**: reverse it immediately as soon as you recognize the counter-productivity generated, and wonders will happen in your life." There is no absolute rule that you have to finish every statement you started. It is not a sign of weakness, but wisdom! We usually are aware that we are saying something pretty negative and counter-productive half-way-thru the statement, yet we keep on speaking nonsense. I understand some citizens make this almost impossible; but do not habitually and subconsciously pre-decide that certain citizens are not worth expressing and empowering positive citizen-interaction skills.

"Cultural differences have an amazing influence on what we believe to be 'acceptable behavior' or 'unacceptable behavior.' How much is prejudice more of a sociocultural influenced behavior than a personal (original-thought) statement? Culture is a major influence on the theories we use to describe and explain sociocultural related behavior. This influences our happiness-anger-sad issues, especially approach and withdrawal behavior." From POLICING PRIVATE PERSONALITIES, Sam Luckey

HOW ARE YOU THINKING

NOT WHAT ARE YOU THINKING

Re-creating, re-energizing and dragging the parts of your past that do not need to be empowered in the present, "present-without-presence." Stuck in the past. We can always intelligently improve **THOUGHTS ABOUT THOUGHTS**, without mentally-imprisoning ourselves and destroying our careers in law-enforcement. We experience a lot of $#%&! Mental distraction safety issues empowered by an undisciplined mind, maladaptive thoughts and emotional issues that eventually and ultimately influence your physical safety behavioral expectations. Out-of-your awareness, weapon-use is becoming more optionally considered during more and more dispatches and traffic stops—you become more **robotic and impersonal** interacting with your community. We easily identify "what" we are thinking, but rarely consider "how" we are thinking—especially our personal decision-making process. Normal thought-process reflection should result in "better-thinking;" occasionally, it merely cements the "thinker" into habitual pre-determined emotional behavioral responses, haphazardly chosen from our emotional library. Philip Tetlock said it best: "We need to cultivate the art of self-overhearing, to learn how to eavesdrop on the mental conversations we have with ourselves." When you describe yourself as "arguing-with-yourself," what do you personally mean by that? Are you just listening in like a third-party?

Are you detecting patterns you are not proud of? Experts state the obvious. We shall actively-listen in as a participant, not as a hostage! How else will you understand if your brain is functioning properly for yourself, the situation you responded to and your community?

"Neuronal pathways as directed 'energy' attached to particular memories—strengthened by the way we talk to ourselves—our internal dialogue. Our ability to 'imagine possible events' has positive and negative potential and consequences. Cognitive processes relying on the 'physiology-of-perception—which is not immune from illusion, delusion and intentional mis-manipulation misperceptions." From POLICING PRIVATE PERSONALITIES, Sam Luckey

The "conditions" (personal, law-enforcement and social) that you continuously find yourself habitually in, are the "effect" of your previous "thoughts" as "cause." "Change your thoughts" and you will change your citizen-interaction. Just as important as neurons are for neural communication, it turns out that the insulation protecting your nerves influences the speed and effectiveness of inter-brain communication processing. Your brain is primed to verify exactly what your **perceptual expectations** have been programmed to "believe" over actual reality. Do you consciously intend "irrational thoughts"? Or do they leak out habitually from your subconscious without your intent and authority? The powerful influence of your subconscious works out of your awareness on any problem you have, any worry you energize, whether based in reality or not. Whether helpful or not. Real associative values or false unrelated values, especially misperceptions, even destructive thoughts. What subtle suggestions do you cultivate in your impersonal and non-subjective subconscious that are false, but subconsciously processed or intuited as truths? This is how we can be self-**hypnotized** into believing and performing false suggestions. As powerful as your subconscious mind is, it cannot reason, or choose to examine a belief before it thrusts false beliefs into your conscious awareness. Beliefs, **even false beliefs** are programmed as true into your subconscious—executing them into your conscious automatically! Every suggestion you make to your subconscious is received as truth, even self-destructive or socially-destructive ways of thinking.

"Habit hierarchies, internal conflicts, even repressed conflicts complicate your primary (innate) drives and secondary (learning by association) drives. ATTITUDES BECOME PERSONALITIES! Out of your awareness, the influence of unconscious motivation, judgments and intentions, alter and manipulates your 'deductive-reasoning' and decision-making skills." From POLICING PRIVATE PERSONALITIES, Sam Luckey

SUB-CONSCIOUS PREDICTIONS TRIAL AND ERROR

Your subconscious does not promote "preferences" between potentialities. Investing mental-energy into understanding what the next moment may present to us, for accuracy, requires that we understand the **immediate past.** Life may be **"lived-forward,"** but it must be bathed in pre-programmed intelligent behavior—especially when we face novel stimuli forces, and must invent or improvise new successful behaviors. Professional cultural transmission of expectations and judgments, are not always based in truth. During a simple police-citizen interaction, both parties may empower representation manipulation, competition, randomness, abstract pattern detection, and convergent thinking—and still mutually agree to a successful de-escalation strategy. Healthy human thought-processes include conscious **introspective "trial and error,"** self-analysis creativity and improvisation, just prior to "commitment" speaking or behaving in a certain way. Once your novel solution is publicly announced or initiated—you will have to monitor how exactly the "others" you are dealing with, interpreted your intended meaningful noises. New information, no standard

53

response and situational fluctuation may require new context after you already spent considerable effort and time behaving in a manner influenced by the past context. A police-officer **hesitating in situational analysis**, desperate to develop a plan, will rely on pre-programmed past experience intelligence gained—subconscious predictions. A plan that falls apart will still require committed "rejection" of that plan, or you will hesitate and doubt the new plan. Thinking about the old plan at the wrong times.

"Our study of personality will yield different results if we only study the psychopathological side of humanity, instead of the successful, creative, and self-actualized members of humanity. Especially those who cross artificial socio-cultural barriers in self-empowerment. In the 'field-of-personality,' should we study the 'personality,' or 'the-person?' Should we study the 'person,' or the 'situation?' Should we study the 'situation,' or the social-environment?'" From POLICING PRIVATE PERSONALITIES, Sam Luckey

IMAGIINING MULTIPLE SCENARIOS

Who programmed your inflexible **pre-programmed** "bonds-of-instinctive" behaviors when dealing with citizen "unpredictability"? At the scene of a crime, you may alternate between *"convergent-thinking"* and *"divergent-thinking."* Do police-officers develop *"stereotyped-behaviors"* as patterns "others" can predict and use against us. Unpredictability infects all of us differently. Dogs and their "sensory-templates" seem better at detecting meaning from a human's non-verbal body language, than humans can. Situational habitual cue-analysis is not always obvious to a police-officer searching for meaning in a community of circumstance modification—where we do not have all the information we would like to have. Most of us, out-of-our awareness; are evolutionarily designed to need to know what "others" are thinking in our effort to understand our **situational awareness** "what-me-worry," non-stop mental chatter. Your intelligence attributes and a creative imagination, needs to be tempered by actual productivity as a quality of success, especially when involving unique situations. How professional are you at "imagining multiple scenarios?" Slowly, rookies become better and better at identifying "remote-analogies" and social-relationship cause and effects, that lead to creative and useful de-escalation techniques. Innovative behaviors work well because they are built on previous elements, deductive logic and novel combinations appropriate for police-work.

"We are evolutionarily designed to neuronally make (predictive coding) behavioral predictions for immediate and future experience—all based on our past experience, as it was neuronally stored and later retrieved. Another way to look at your personality essence and its influence on your behavior is to consider that you are 'being-personality,' instead of the point-of-view that your 'doing-personality.' The REAL YOU behaving as 'BEING PERSONALITY.' The façade-personality is revealed when you are 'DOING PERSONALITY.'" From POLICING PRIVATE PERSONALITIES, Sam Luckey

WE ARE SOCIAL PRIMATES—INTELLIGENT IMPROVISATION AND SITUATIONAL AWARENESS

How much of your habitual behavioral response is based on unplanned and counter-productive inferences and expectations in your poorly defined search for *"proximate and ultimate causation"*? **Autosuggestion** can be programmed into your subconscious, the good and the bad; receptive language skills verified through productive language skills, as we are social-primates. Simply noticing stimuli while on patrol will require some degree of **"controlled thought or observation"** for the stimuli to trigger full-awareness development of innovative behaviors. Once in our awareness, the stimuli may trigger multiple alternate interpretations in our search for meaning, the role of memory; heavily influenced by subliminal-priming that we may not be aware of. **Situational specific reactions** influenced by instinctive behavior or learned behavior, include a thought process—even if you are not aware of it. Sensory ambiguity encourages mental processing that "fills-in the details" for us, right or wrong, our search for common purpose. We auto-construct mental-model cortical reflexes, influenced by both what we know, and what we do not know—yet. Memories you carry and activate are neuronally processed as "current sensory input," that may prioritize the wrong conclusions, including categorical perceptions based on "suggestions" that you may not even be aware of. We can continue **anticipating potentialities** (intelligent improvisation), while thinking about the stimuli in question after we have departed, utilizing multiple sensory modalities to clear any doubt we have—patrolling in purposeful ambiguity.

"Are you open to eliminating some of your negative habitual behaviors? Are you open to learning or developing positive and productive behaviors? Who is stopping you? Self or Other? From POLICING PRIVATE PERSONALITIES, Sam Luckey

We must clearly understand the consequences of our own behavioral choices. Did you perceive reality as it really is, or did you merely modify your anticipations to see what you expected. Expectation conditioned situational awareness. Observing stimuli does not guarantee that you actually noticed that stimuli, especially if you are distracted out of the here-and-now—**your sensory-templates** can be easily ignored out of your awareness without intent. When you initiate "action-physical-behavior," you have expectations built into your behavior. Mindless counter-productive behavior can become a **chain of behaviors** rather easily and aggressively. Is your purposeful behavior sense-of-self really what you intended? Your behavioral response as *"spatiotemporal patterns"* involving certain muscle activation as patterns of timing, strength, duration and neuronal feedback. How much of your "planning" for future events, is merely based on an unconsciously stored ambiguous intent you did not know you possessed or empowered? Novel encounters require assemblage planning and "goal-plus-feedback" verification. Sometimes we are influenced by **burned-out police-officers** (excitation transfer or negative work habits) and all their pre-programmed verbal-conditioning, counteracting positive autosuggestions. They unconsciously want you to be as unhappy and negative as they are.

"You can be obsessed without compulsiveness, if you are also obsessed with doubt. Experiencing just enough doubt in what you seek, preventing compulsiveness from over powering your expression of behavior—so far." POLICING PRIVATE PERSONALITIES, Sam Luckey

PRIMED IMPRESSIONS AND JUDGMENTS

Sometimes police-officers have to "act" a behavior to get the citizens full attention. The effect of **"implicit-memory"** in your behavioral responses at complicated incidents, should always be modified and energized by your on-the-scene developing **"explicit memory."** Your unconscious influences what police-officers "embrace and reject," especially your approach and withdrawal behaviors. Your "conscious-explainer" can "justify" just about anything—good and bad, even imagined events as factual! The mental model you construct is your prime satisfaction stability determinant—over the reality of the situation you responded to. To satisfy your erroneous mental-model, you will neuronally auto-fill-in details, anything, real or imagined. Your memory provides the context, categorization and comprehension for sight and sound suggestibility and interpreted conclusions. Becoming an accurate intelligent "passionate-observer," is not a sign of weakness. Improvising police-officers "present-with-presence" at all novel-situations. It is a necessary step between sensation and behavioral action; muscle movement as spatio-temporal patterns trapped in time. Think about what you like and prefer, on the job and off. Did these ambiguous preferences originally arise unconsciously and unchallenged? Acting includes nonverbal behavior. **Physiological arousal** can rarely be hidden. Science has proven that **cultural stereotypes** are culturally transmitted—especially values attributed. Your own thought processes may be giving "others" control over your body and mind, that you may be unaware of. You end up making their thoughts, your thoughts. You may be relying on wandering inefficient subconscious memory searches to "answer" all questions you have been primed to believe, based on "others'" opinions, not yours. You are not arguing with your subconscious; you are consciously arguing with all the input from others (thoughts, impressions and imagery) you passively allowed to be programmed into your subconscious—which operates 24 hours a day. Your actions do evil deeds, not your mind. Your emotional expressions are primarily automatic and involuntary—making them more believable than artificial or crafted facial expressions. Be careful with your "verdicts and conclusions." Scientists have proven in what they nicknamed "two unrelated experiments," that your "experience" right before clinicians determine "impressions and judgments" you hold about someone, are "primed" and influenced by the unrelated prior experience—without your awareness of such influence. Even new situations. Think of all the "prior-experience" you bring to every dispatch you respond to.

CONSCIOUS-FIRST ASSUMPTION IS JUST AN ASSUMPTION

CONSCIOUS FIRST (JUST AN ASSUMPTION)

Your "culture" also influences your unconscious behavioral responses to life—especially your social identity. Even "police" culture! What cultural identity are your children being groomed for? How much do your **thoughts interpret your experience** for you or against you? Recognize that when unfulfilled desire is frustrating, do not be or "do" "frustrated." If you **habitually have certain thoughts**, they must be positive for you, right? You would not recognize habitual self or socially destructive thoughts and not correct these thoughts—would you? Recognition is the first step. When your subconscious mind acts as a "healer" for yourself and your citizen-interaction, consciously analyze what your subconscious automatically promotes onto your world. It is obvious that we should not let a prior citizen-interaction that we found offending, infecting our behavior, stay alive in our head for days or weeks. Attention is the key. Sometimes we reignite and energize old memories that are not worth reliving over and over. Patrolling in "**heightened irritability**." A "mood" that everyone recognizes in your behavior. Are your "motivation-states" controlled by your "emotional-states?" It has been proven that antidepressant medications actually help compulsive shoppers, refrain. In an experiment concerning consumer behaviorism, simply putting a pro-healthy eating sign on the entrance door, resulted in consumers actually buying less garbage food products. You are as subject **to beliefs and suggestions** as the citizens you engage with. Recognize what the outside world programs into your subconscious— especially misattribution effects. Sometimes beliefs are really just thoughts. Your motivation and evaluation skills are not just based on conscious processes. Your behavioral processes primarily initiate automatically from unconscious mental programs—not really guided by conscious awareness as much as we would like to believe. Dr. Baugh describes how he had to overcome his "**conscious-first assumption**" towards behavioral processes. Our undisciplined thought processes spend too much time in the past and the future—instead of here/now awareness.

EMOTIONAL MIND—RAPID AROUSAL LEVELS

As your career in law-enforcement continues, you should at least have less anxiety distracting you from the here-and-now. Some experts report that "**self-affirmations**" of your skills and intentions

59

(interpersonal effectiveness), before and during stressful situations, help many in law-enforcement. Take control of your thoughts (emotional regulation) instead of allowing your (distorted) thoughts to control you. Would someone you work alongside describe you as possessing "inflexible and extreme characteristics," potentially an **"impulse control** disorder," or "stress response syndrome." Which would be more effective for you? "Letting go of your emotions," or, "learning to manage your emotions?" The ability to process and reason your emotional turmoil is required to prevent instability. You do not really understand yourself, if you do not understand and control your emotional displays and subsequent emotional thought processes. There are positive aspects to your emotional mind. Are your thoughts (based on emotion) generating a counter-productive state or condition of mind (mood disorders/affective disorders)? How rapid are your "rapid arousal levels?" Law-enforcement feels justified in energizing the faulty-belief system that convinces us that circumstances are generating incompatible citizen-interaction, not our own undisciplined thought-processes. When you leave a complicated incident, do you only **"extrapolate" mental me-me-me**, (validation) look what happened to me?

"Experts remind us that our behavior concerns our beliefs about reality. Our behavior does not reflect a 'function-of-reality.' To keep bad thoughts and malicious intent alive in our head, usually requires 'volitional-effort' – 'an active-primary-causal-force!' Emotional significance is a major influence on approach and withdrawal behavior. Biological predisposition and your arousal level may influence more than the actual situation. Expectations are very personal, and personally empowered. Stimulus recognition does not mean you are conscious of the stimulus." From POLICING PRIVATE PERSONALITIES, Sam Luckey.

EMERGENCY BEHAVIORAL ALTERATION

Do you trust all your personal-agenda biased subconscious "impulses" that arise randomly without conscious intent? You may find it easier to ignore impulses that should be ignored, by removing the urge, rather than stopping the urge. The future does not exist right now. Remain in relationship to what is actually occurring here/now. Always remain aware that subcortical movement coordination may occur out of your awareness—relying on **pre-determined** sequential spatio-temporal activity, pre-programmed also out of your awareness. Did you really plan on that "delayed-response," or were you experiencing mental short-circuited decision-making? A police-officer making emergency behavioral alteration on-the-fly, requires a team effort involving the premotor and prefrontal cortex, cognitive analysis and instant decision-making skills. Your intention-skills influence whether your intended movement requires behavioral alterations based on timing issues; if your auto-behavioral response was even appropriate, or memory failed when you needed it. Cognition can occur out of your awareness, influenced by your mood or when carrying a negative personal-agenda out into the community. Your response to "difficulty" is personally empowered and usually flavored by "priming" influences you may not be aware of. Having multiple behavioral-actions available, does' not guarantee "fluid-behavior," when multiple actions are auto-chained into a police response.

"Sociocultural domination has even altered our personal definitions of 'human-being.' Most of us see it translated into personal mentalese as 'human-object.' We see 'everything' as 'things.' We need to be reminded constantly that 'being' in 'human-being' means 'activity,' 'human-activity' experience—existence not as an object. Seeing humans as 'beings,' not as objects, will make empathy and compassion more primary than secondary human events. The on-going human 'being' process-activity meaning-making moment-by-moment creation, until we are the last person to die in our lifetime.

What good are 'perceptions' and 'sensory-information' without 'meaning-making context?'" From POLICING PRIVATE PERSONALITIES, Sam Luckey.

AUTOMATIC EVALUATIVE ATTITUDES

Police-intelligence includes "comparing-of-relationships," out in the community, when dealing with a non-compliant citizen. Neutralizing can be more effective than merely stopping conflicts. Sometimes moving with an opponent, is easier than stopping the opponent, because you can merge, even contribute to and direct your opponents flow of energy and movement, with yours. While moving with the opponent, you are fully engaged and aware. **Reading the other's intent**, acting before something happens, is a skill you need in law-enforcement. How mature and secure is your **relationship with "change?"** There is a "Field of **Attitude Research**," that includes "automatic-evaluative-attit2udes." In police-citizen interaction, we both determine/evaluate each other (**predicting behavior**), initially from subconscious mental processes, our evaluative skills concerning the other in our life at that moment. More senior police-officers have cultivated their evaluative skills over the years, becoming a trustworthy intuitive base for initial contact. These evaluative skills are hard to teach a rookie, especially if the instructors rookie training-shift is just backed up dispatches of chaos. This **intuitive evaluation** may also imply that "strong/urgent attitudes" as feelings, identify what stimuli you should immediately focus your attention on—police-behavior. Humans have advanced analysis of outside-stimuli and external events from simple observation, to the ability to quietly in our own head; analyze potential actions instead of habitual-actions, and further rehearse these alternatives, choose the best option, improve the quality of that choice, and recognize immediately if our "plan" hits speed-bumps or needs revision. We may need to "kill" that plan and regroup—which can be very hard for law-enforcement motivated and ready to "pounce!" Training and on-the-job experience is your research mental-library. Intelligent solutions that work, seem occasionally to develop thought-wise in milliseconds, but don't count on it—intelligent survival. During a complicated dispatch, your memories alongside sensations determine your thoughts, and hopefully you only express the best ones? Dr. William H. Calvin reminds police-officers that: "<u>Thoughts are movements that have not happened yet</u>, (and maybe never will). They're fleeting and mostly ephemeral."

"Emergency use of your weapon as 'programmed-movement,' may be 'motor-programmed' by 'open-loop' control mental processes; meaning that 'motor-commands' are pre-structured to the point that there is no 'feedback" or 'error-detection' available until it is too late, you have fired your weapon. 'Rapid-skilled-actions,' once initiated, involving open-loop control motor performance by design, do not allow real-time modifications—what will happen has happened! Cognitive scientists consider "triggered-reflexes" as being too fast to be classified "voluntary" reactions. Visual and auditory interference is a real concern that also "distorts judgments." From POLICING PRIVATE PERSONALITIES SAM LUCKEY

SELF MANIPULATING MODELS OF REALITY

"Conflicts of Representation," and the incorrect attitude evaluation of citizens you encounter, may also encourage you to express more positive, calm and worry-free attitudes, when you should have been more cautious and alert. Armed with a weapon does not guarantee that your "**expression-of-attitude**" is appropriate and well-thought out! The best way to explain a field-sobriety test is to model every step. In modern society, your unconscious determines your calmness or alertness more than it really should. Nowadays, older adults are just as likely as a teen to try to ruin your day. Your stored "likes" and "dislikes" may have a detrimental effect on honest and well-intended evaluation. We can manipulate models of reality in our own head and miss when the red light changed to green.

Neutral, more relaxed police-citizen encounters usually do not require quick initial evaluation, as our thought-processes are calmly extracting more information from the encounter. Scientist investigating human evaluative attitude research, use the term **"attitude-objects"** to describe stimuli they use in their investigations. "Regulars," citizens we have professional encounters on a regular-basis, may become "attitude-obje2cts" that we mentally allow to self-entrap ourselves in police-behavior that we regret. Some police-officers deteriorate into **"objects-of-attitude!"** Around the world, I remember on some complicated emotional incidents, I hoped that certain other police-officers would not respond—and make things worse! Synaptic strength may be the only reason you chose a counter-productive behavioral response; which, if negative factors are ignored, may become a near-permanent filter infecting "long-term-potentiation," a less positive "sense-of-self." Passive "memory-resonation" may become a nagging distraction bias leading to wrong-decisions, choices and conclusions.

"You are more than your perceptions; you can actually intend to do something 'maturely' with them, rather than letting your perceptions dictate your experience and happiness. Carl Jung described the meeting between two personalities as similar to the mixing of two chemical substances, creating both a reaction and a transformation. Add situational influences, behavioral inconsistencies, unique individual psychophysical systems and known or unknown psychopathologies to our interactions, and things get interesting. Albert Einstein lamented that we no longer recognize the gift of our 'intuitive-mind,' because sociocultural indoctrination and expectation prefers the 'rational-mind.' Is it possible that your mind is so efficient, that it believes it is your body? Your mind alters direction perception!" From POLICING PRIVATE PESONALITIES, Sam Luckey

ATTITUDES BECOME PERSONALITIES

Attitude/evaluative clinical investigations developed a process called "**affective priming paradigm.**" "Priming" is the keyword. We may not want to believe it, but they have proven that your "experience" with outside stimuli, just prior to your encounter requiring police evaluative mental skills, is influencing, if not determining your evaluative processing of stimuli you are about to encounter—becoming judge and jury. "Priming-forces" may determine your success at de-escalation, more than the situation. Police-attitudes become police-personalities. Your memory, out of your awareness, has determined facts that will not be evaluated or questioned any further. You carried what researcher Bob Zajonc called, "**feeling without thinking!**" You carried certain "attitudes" about the upcoming citizen-interaction as subconscious-fact, influencing your citizen-encounter, more than the actual reality of the citizen-encounter. Citizens carry certain "attitudes" about the upcoming police-interaction as subconscious-fact, influencing their police-encounter, more than the actual reality of the police-encounter. Imagine your department put out a yearbook for every year you worked in law-enforcement. What brief "quotes" would co-workers write about you—year-after-year. Extract quotes indicating your "**attitude" and "personality,**" year-after- year. Are those quotes you would appreciate being identified with thyself? Are you positively evolving during your wild trip in law-enforcement, year-after-year, or de-evolving, perhaps behavior that is going to get yourself arrested? Do you really want to be incarcerated and have "others" modify your "attitude?"

While performing self-neuroplasticity on yo8urself, remain aware of the potential that your good-intentions may dig up dirt on "yourself." Bad thoughts you have forgotten may return to conscious awareness. Certain citizens that "always" piss-you-off, will become up-front thought patterns, which unfortunately, may be "**priming**" thyself for the wrong-reasons, contaminating your next citizen-encounter. It does not require "conscious-effort" to "prime" (unconscious-programming that you activated) the wrong "attitude" for you; and the wrong attitude evaluative assessment of the citizen or police-officer you are approaching, for your next citizen-encounter or police-encounter. Primed police attitudes become police personalities, infecting not just rookies, but the entire community. It is important to recognize that "priming" evaluative attitudes unconsciously "thought" just prior to police-citizen interaction, is just as easily, **"primed" by** "objects in the real world," not just humanity. The "habit" you have of touching your pistol handgrip, or unsnapping the holster for easier access as you approach the citizen, is that **"priming-habit" or "habit-priming**?" Are you immune to infective and counterproductive aspects of priming?

"Do you have any idea who you really are (identity-formation or identity-crisis?), because you are basically a 'socially-constructed-self' of no real-individual-identity, substance and lacking a genuine persona? This is especially true for many in law-enforcement who seem to have no 'off-duty' personality or self—they are only 'law-enforcement.' Other than socio-cultural mandates, you have no real personal interests, desires and goals. Is 'culture' the biggest influence on your personality? Is your 'permanence-of-personality' the personality you would have chosen if you knew you had a choice? How much does a description of someone's personality— really reflect his or her environment? From POLICING PRIVATE PERSONALITIES, Sam Luckey

EVALUATE-EVALUATE-EVALUATE

It is hard to evaluate your own unconscious programming from a conscious perspective. To be clear, you may have no knowledge or idea about the person you are about to interact with, other than self-stored (correctly associated?) past-experience "priming" interpreted/evaluated by you when it was stored, and interpreted/evaluated by you when it rises to conscious attention.

What cognitive psychologist John Bargh calls **"unconscious evaluation of everything**." Police-officers have to "evaluate" their whole shift! Unconscious priming began as a primitive behavior, that must have more benefit than detriment—I hope, to continue such powerful unconscious influence on modern daily life. Humans have the unconscious ability, clinically proven, to automatically push away what our unconscious considers as our dislikes/bad stuff, and similarly as an unconscious process, pull closer what we like and dislike. Even the speed of your response is influenced by (good/bad) "priming." Before we have time to attentionally evaluate at the conscious level, our body has responded one-way for good stuff and one-way for bad stuff. Approach and withdrawal behavior we do thousands of times a week.

THEORY OF MIND

SUPPOSITIONS AND ASSOCIATIONS

Think about the last time you had a suspect leaning over your car, while you do a quick weapon safety pat-down. What "priming" issues did you bring to the situation? Did they interfere with or improve officer safety issues and further understanding what situational attention has presented to you? At the conscious awareness/attention level? At the unconscious awareness/attention level—how would you know? We need to remember that "**feature-detection**" is reliant on unconsciously designed categorization skills. Now think back to the last time you discovered a suspicious item or hidden weapon during a search. Did it catch you off-guard because the last twenty times you searched someone you found nothing? Happened to me several times. It still bothers me how distracted/confused I was for a couple seconds. My **predictive assessment** "priming" differed from the reality of the situation. Police-officers, routinely interact with a citizen experiencing a syndrome referred to as "Jamais vu," where a weapon you find on them or in their car; a weapon you know they

67

are "familiar" with, they claim to be unfamiliar with. Your subconscious mind has more control over your muscles than you realize. How long did it take you to accept the dramatic change to your situational attentional assessment? What did unconscious "priming" contribute to your behavioral response? Practice making **situational assessments** as soon as you safely can, to become more aware of the infection prior experience has on your unconscious "priming." Develop and understand what you learned, to share with the next rookie you assist in training—or a burned-out veteran. Every year, we lose a lot of knowledge that had to be learned the hard way on some rough shifts, that was not shared with co-workers before quitting, retiring or dying. Is your current "theory-of-mind," contributing to effective citizen interaction? When your "attention" is distracted, what part of you is paying attention (suppositions and associations) to what is needed at that moment? "Meaning," especially face and object recognition, cannot be separated from experience—associative memory for law-enforcement needs to be appropriate and helpful.

SELF-DEFEATING NEGATIVE THOUGHTS

Sometimes during law-enforcement responses to violent incidents, law-enforcement presenting a well-trained calm-attentive helping-attitude, remaining emotionless, pisses off the citizen we are interacting with. They would love for you to get as out of control as they are. Instead, we "always" remain calm and emotionless; which will improve your overall emotional health and citizen-interaction, always a step in the right direction, **self-neuroplasticity motivation**. Goals, objectives and truly understanding your personal reason for wanting to initiate attitude and personality "change," will need to be clearly defined. The more you believe in this need for change, the more effective self-neuroplasticity will occur with the power of your unconscious always responding to concrete defined goals.

Your undisciplined non-stop thought processes self-neuroplasticize your brain in self-defeating ways—supplied by memory—which negative thoughts reformulate back into your memory, over-and-over-and over. Every moment of your life, **experience is modifying your brain.** When you are experiencing negative counter-productive thoughts during citizen-interaction, do these negative thoughts require "volitional-effort" to suppress, alter or change? Is it possible that you are unconsciously "affirming" these negative thoughts, locking you into behavior you recognize as inappropriate? Stress in law-enforcement is a given, almost appropriate for such a challenging job. It is the inappropriate stress that gets you, especially if it leads to excessive self-criticism. In law-enforcement, it is not always your emotions that trigger improper counter-productive behavior. When **"crossing-the-line" becomes habitual and routine;** someday your unconscious will take control and "behave" as programmed, while your conscious-self impotently screams **"why am I doing this!"** You will be responsible for what unconscious habitual pre-programming created.

NEGATIVE IDEATION HABITUATION

Other police-officers are also efficient triggers for improper police-behavior—habitual undisciplined suggestions, joking remarks and "interceding sensory stimulus." While on patrol, which mental process empowers your personal "causal-force," when actively focusing-attention on outside stimuli? **"Attention-as-effect?"** The "stimuli" caught your visual-attention and you automatically focused your attention? Or, you unconsciously scanned your field-of-vision as an "active-primary" causal-force—you already empowered "attention-focus" before detecting outside-stimuli specific for your intentions at that moment. Police are routinely bombarded by multiple-outside-stimuli at the same time, challenging our mental processing resources even more while **"focusing-attention."** It is important for you to identify your personal neural mechanism response to stimuli in relation to your focus-of-attention. You are not born with a limited life-time number of neurons dedicated to differing levels for processing your attention-skills. Use it for strengthening neuronal-based positive mental programs; or, your synaptic strengths will be replaced by more routine negative ideation habituation. Mentally exercise your positive focus-of-attention skills, without the influence of your negative focus-of-attention skills.

"What are some psychological forces that make you unique? Outside of conscious-awareness is where most of your personality resides in waiting. Waiting for social-interaction to disclose bits and pieces, especially attitudes and preoccupations that you cannot seem to let go of. Be careful with your conscious and unconscious intentions, desires, needs, wants and motivations. They intentionally and unintentionally create and empower your self-preprogrammed destiny—with or without your awareness or permission. Are all of the behavioral patterns associated with you and your personality— are they behavioral labels you really want reinforced and identified with you? One short, to the point definition of personality is 'potentialities-for-action.' Is your 'sense-of-self, just a short ambiguous always-changing thought? From POLICING PRIVATE PERSONALITIES, Sam Luckey.

NEURAL REPRESENTATION COMPETITION

Human neural-representation limits police skills at monitoring multiple outside-stimuli at the same time. Every object clearly in your visual-field is competing for your limited neural-representation processing capabilities. We are only human. Every object, sound, smell, visual-processing, internal fears, worries and pains—all compete for your limited neural-representation capabilities, **seeking sacred-conscious awareness**. Outside stimuli as "input" influencing your approach and withdrawal behavior, happiness or sad, excitatory or inhibitory, into your brain—creating an "impulse." Associative memories critical for police-work, rely on this "input" cerebral cortex processing; which includes all the sensory modalities at play in your head, influenced by moods, cares, obligations, relationships and preoccupations. Circumstance situational readjustment in competition with habitual emotional responses and instinctive genetic predispositions—current sensory inputs camouflaged by all your pre-determined imaginary mental imagery. Unconscious and unverified mental facts-on-file may behaviorally motivate you into unverified "**chains-of-inferences**," not applicable for your here/now situation. Your investigative plan is processed in between "instinctive-wisdom" and "sterile deduction," a near predatory search for truth, more than simple curiosity.

"Most of your 'stimulus-response-behaviors' are made without conscious attention or awareness—they are automated in your unconscious, based on piss-poor-prior-pre-programming. Take control of your attention-skills, because 'where attention goes, energy flows.' From POLICING PRIVATE PERSONALITIES, Sam Luckey

ABSENCE-OF ATTENTION

INDIFFERENT POLICE-ROBOTIC PATROLING

Neuroscientists warn police-officers that every object in your field-of-vision, competes for your limited-neural-representation. Intend that the most valuable at that moment outside stimuli competing for your attention, are the ones that actually get your attention skills activated. Unfortunately, a police-officers attention-focusing skills need to accurately and timely, understand multiple specific "**strength-of-the-stimulus**," visual-field analysis—especially involving critical-incidents. We "assume" that the most **threatening stimulus** will be identified and provide sufficient neural-representation to get our attention. Selective focus-of-attention based on your unconscious "association-skills," may not always reflect your behavioral-modification—you are still distracted by "novel," colorful, and moving outside-stimuli. It is just as important to skillfully and timely disengage from unimportant, distracting and unrelated outside-stimuli, as it is to focus attention on the intended. Simply stated; stronger neuron activation for intended focusing attention, and decreased neuron activation for unrelated stimuli. Neuroscientists have proven that we have specialized neurons responding to faces, color and even movement. Your response to outside stimuli is your brain's response—your interest at that time is a major influence on what stimuli you focus on. You can recognize outside stimuli out of your conscious awareness— even misidentify objects and threat-levels. This is why you never respond to an incident as a pissed-off distracted pre-programmed "absence-of-attention" indifferent police-robot.

"Prior experience and learned 'patterns-of-responses' become unconsciously motivated 'patterns-of-behavior,' and are not always positive. You cannot prevent your experience from changing your brain and neural processes—every second of your life. You may not be able to prevent the change, but you can be aware of it." From Policing Private Personalities, Sam Luckey

ATTENTION SKILLS MODIFY YOUR BRAIN

Dr. Swartz points out what should be obvious to all of us; "Paying attention" as a "property-of-the-mind," "determines the activity of the brain." Practice modulating your neuronal functions by simply using "directed-attention." Searching for a suspect who fled on-foot late at night into a housing area—hopefully you have already fine-tuned your attention-focus and disengage-focus skills. Staring into a darkened non-descript field, without even recognizing any stimuli, still increases neuronal activation for neurons responsible for that area of "nothing." Your "primed" expectations, "focusing-on-a-specific-attribute," real-or-imagined, will cause neurons activation to spike. Your **expectations** can "prime" your brain to auto-activate a "greater response," than if you were not "primed" in advance.

This is why police-training needs to include recognizing and analyzing your emotional/feeling processing learned-habits, not just during complicated incidents; but, all the influences of personality and attitude that preceded your arrival. Your attention skills are spread out over multiple brain-processing sites. "Divided-attention" at the wrong time for a police-officer, can get you killed. Attention for a police-officer influences neuronal-activation on the stimulus in-question. We need to be aware that increased neuronal-activation in one area of your brain, usually means other sense-based neuronal areas experience decreased neuronal activity. Are those the sense-based experience you really want decreased, if not deleted out of your awareness? Your attention-skills modify the physical structure of your brain!

"Some neuroscientists report clinical data that indicates humans have a 'automatic appraisal mechanism.' For it to be an unconscious 'automatic' response involving motor-pre-programming, this requires past (memory) experience, as 'input,' 'programming,' expectations and judgments." From POLICING PRIVATE PERSONALITIES, Sam Luckey

UNINTENDED STIMULI-ASSOCIATION

PATTERN DETECTION SITUATIONAL PREDICTIONS

Do you just end up patrolling bored, inattentive and vulnerable, from "innate-programming alone?" You don't go out of your way or self-initiate for community or your department? Do your immediate previous mental processes contaminate or improve your present presence. We have all tried to forget something horrible, visual, audio, smell; yet, we had to overcome the natural human ability to neuronally re-excite what we would really prefer to not re-excite— those same thoughts. The speed of our thought processes is a blessing. For the undisciplined police-officer, novel negative correlates not based on the reality of the situation you responded to. A police-officers in-the-community "experimental-predictions," "plans-of-action," and "pattern-detections" should be more than confident guesses. The tone and order we ask questions is just as important as the sequencing of questions, coupled with how we pose the question. Are the primitive-prototype categories and context of your unconscious knowledge base—up-to-date? Are you sure your linguistic skills actually communicate to those listening—what you consciously intend? Not unconscious programming that you have never verified, especially unintended stimuli associations.

"Julien Jaynes described that our trust in language as a solid-dictionary based communication process, was really a 'rampant restless sea of metaphor.' The more familiar the metaphor, the more we 'feel' we understand. Can you be self-conscious without the influence of memory and patterns-of meaning? Experts remind us that as much as 95% of your 'learning' occurs out of your awareness. Attachments to your thoughts effect and infect the body. Your mind, 'the maker of judgments.' Remember that last sentence and you have also made a new judgment and new memory! Controlling our thoughts is a different mental process than controlling your 'inner-reactions' to those same thoughts. Habits are 'learned-aspects' of behavior. Have you ever intentionally created an 'effective-habit?' From POLICING PRIVATE PERSONALITIES, Sam Luckey

YOU ARE A SENTIENT BEING

Proactive behavioral inhibition is a different mental process than inhibiting thoughts that lead to improper police-behavior. To be truly proactive in eliminating police-behaviors that are going to eventually get you into serious trouble, you have to pre-plan. **Serious pre-planning** requires you to face every unconscious habit and impulse towards violence that you have. It will not matter how you school yourself—if your unconscious still holds incompatible, biased or racist beliefs, your unconscious will program your conscious behavior for you. Don't wait until a violent emotional incident to decide immediately a plan of action is needed to de-escalate your own improper behavior. You are always empowered as a "sentient being," to choose to not get into these questionable situations—that you seem to find yourself in a lot. Your body's motor-programming operates predominately from the unconscious. Motor movements that would not occur without pre-programming from "experience." Unconscious control and "activation" of your body's movement further empowers the unconscious, because genetics and unconscious forces determined the schematic or configuration purposes, strengths and weaknesses—especially recognizing repair needs—out of your conscious awareness. Unconscious processes predominately categorized and contextualized the **importance-amplification** of the world for you. The most distracted individuals will usually be saved from injury only because of unconscious "this is important-amplification" alert systems auto-activating body behavior for us.

"Police-officers have to be aware that your unconscious detects many things out of your conscious awareness. Your unconscious may have detected danger and be neuronally screaming watch out while your conscious mind may be distracting your awareness out of the present moment. We are evolutionarily designed to determine the intentions of others, especially any 'goal-directed-action.' Have you 'become-your-reflexes,' instead of just having reflexes? We are stimulus-response creatures!" From *POLICING PRIVATE PERSONALITIES, Sam Luckey*

PROGRAMMED BEHAVIORAL RESPONSE

Out of your awareness; evolutionarily tested and modified, natural adaptive brain mechanisms developed to deal with the variability and dangerousness of our environment—unconsciously configured by whom? There is even a field of science called "population-biology" which should have some helpful information pertinent to police-citizen interaction. Have you ever run a self-diagnostic neocortical-connectivity episodic memory evaluation? No. Maybe your unconscious does it for you—but never reveals the results to your conscious-self, until it is self-evident and obvious that something is wrong? Have you behaved criminally yet? Ambiguous visual perceptions can be recognized before initiating a behavioral response. Ambiguous mental processing—out of our awareness—will initiate behavioral responses as programmed. Neuroscientists evaluating brain scans have to determine if what displayed indicates **"reduced excitability" or Increased inhibition**," a key factor for treatment options. I'd like to see a clinical experiment designed where the respondent can only act on or answer questions with "reduced excitability" or "increased inhibition."

CONTROLLED DISORDER COMMUNITY RESONANCE

A cognitive neuroscientist whose books I enjoy reading, William H. Calvin, summarized a variation of **chaos-theory**, synapses, neuromodulators and brain processes that influence your skills at **"shifting-your-attention."** I found the associations he identified, oddly relatable to a routine patrol for law-enforcement. Imagine you are having a very-rough shift; your "community" seems to be in total "chaos!" Your citizen-interaction results in unusually strong negative feedback. Your skills at pre-detecting behavioral patterns are finding "predictions," "pre-planning" and "counter-measures," are difficult to design and implement in a timely—efficient productive manner. Complicated citizen behavior patterns that look behaviorally-random, are not really random. "Chaos on steroids" is not returning to normal "chaos;" a randomness that weirdly seems welcome, relaxing and refreshing to you. Simple "chaos" is a shift that you "understand" and can relate more calmly with—perhaps, "controlled-disorder"? You more seriously analyze and mentally investigate the deterministic "underlying-mechanisms" that are producing this extreme-unusually more violent community-chaos. The bad-actors contributing to this extreme chaos, may be considered **"chaotic-attractors."** There is a way for you to bring community "resonance" back to (what is "accepted" to be) "normal." Normal chaotic-resonance—a feeling that you have become accustomed to for that community. You may have to "resonate" with the "chaotic-attractors" in some novel way, in order to defeat them, or implement "relaxation-oscillators" into their behavior. Your attention and awareness skills need to be vigilant, but not so hyper-vigilant that shifting your attention and awareness becomes bogged down in visual-over-stimulation that entraps instead of contributing to community safety. Neuroscientists remind us that even an "unchanging stimulus pattern," that you may experience as viewed from your patrol-car windshield; has the potential to provide conflicting perceptual differences and alternating variations. (Look for illustrations of **"figure-ground-illusions"** for a demonstration of conflicting perceptual differences that appear even as you intend and fixate not to.)

Sometimes your specific pre-learned automatic and habitual behaviors trigger emotional dysregulation. Your personal thought processes influence and activate your personal **mental "defense-system"** against real-life threats and imagined threats. Intend rational responses and conscious decisions instead of habitual involuntary reactions. When your mind "wanders," this can feel natural, nothing really wrong with your mind wandering—unless the timing is inappropriate, distracting and potentially dangerous. When you are frustrated or angry, emotional exaggeration, is this possible without making internal judgements? Can you really recognize feelings of anxiety without identifying the source? Just thinking "sad-thoughts" can create physiological responses, even stress-inducing body damaging hormones.

DISTRESS TOLERANCE SKILLS

Recognizing the emotions that you are experiencing, is the first step in learning to manage them. Your initial reaction to an event is considered a natural reaction, your **"primary emotional response."** It is your secondary emotional reactions that get most law-enforcement in trouble. **Secondary emotions** can be controlled before they become maladaptive behaviors. Experts report that you can regulate your emotions—independent of the situation you responded to. Many self-help books direct the reader to simply **"let-go"** of things that have entrapped our thought processes. Dr. Joseph Murphy reminds us that: "<u>Acceptance is not the same as approval</u>." Acceptance as a form of recognition which will trigger more positive behavioral changes; if this recognition initiates behavioral improvement during police-citizen interaction. When processing emotional and violent incidents, it helps to remember **"the objective of your citizen-interaction."** Some police-officers possess an absolute intolerance for "negotiating." If you are in the right, forms of manipulation are unnecessary. Our feelings seem to be related to what you are thinking at that moment—especially **impulsive behaviors.** You can learn "distress-tolerance skills." Your body may be alerting you that you are becoming emotional, before your mind recognizes what is happening. It is hard to "stay-in-the-moment" when you have dispatches waiting for you to solve this situation ASAP. Proper rationalization and examination of this situation may be negatively influenced by your past experience, especially priming-susceptibility.

POTENTIAL POSITIVE POSSIBLITIES

At first, PTSD was categorized as an anxiety disorder. It was reclassified as "disorders associated with trauma and stressors." PTSD symptoms are considered "your body's natural defense mechanisms to stress." It is hard for soldiers and law-enforcement experiencing PTSD to "distance themselves" from the original traumatic events, because the next shift will bring us back in contact with additional traumatic events. Sometimes it is difficult to "live-in-the-moment," or, conduct **"non-evaluative observation,"** especially self-compassion. Mental health clinicians encourage you to understand that a "lapse" in proper behavioral responses is normal and healthy. It is the **"relapses"** that habitually bring you back into the hopeless negativity of counter-productive thought patterns. PTSD can make you not even consider "viewing things as they are." Potential positive possibilities and potentialities are not recognized, evaluated, nor considered. You are trapped in emotional dysfunction—your thoughts and thinking patterns have been hijacked. What circumstances and subsequent actions do your undisciplined thought processes create? Dr. James Allen reminds us that these "circumstances" you habitually find yourself in, reveal you to yourself. You may attract what you desire, but in reality, you really attract what your behavior and personality attract— habitually! Like an obsessive purposeless **"behavioral magnet!"** Recognize the warning signs that you are "defocusing!" Can you describe the difference between "observed-phenomenon" and "un-observed-phenomenon?" I used to hit rookies with questions like that, implying that the answer is the holy-grail for all police-sciences! You can learn a lot about someone when they choose to ramble-on about subjects they know nothing about.

BEHAVIOR AS A FUNCTION OF THE BRAIN

Do you interact on-the-job with citizens (even other law-enforcement) that have what experts long-ago described as behavioral pathological "disease-of-the-will?" Do you have any positive habits you consciously intend to express? Are your habits all unconscious and ambiguous in nature—behavioral infection improper for police-citizen interaction? It is easier to choose and temper your thoughts, instead of trying to change reality and circumstances that are already physically in perpetual motion. We are supposed to be the "adults" during police-citizen interaction! Are you clear on what you are **"willing" into your life** right now? Purposeless thought creates a purposeless life. Your thoughts determine success and achievement, or unconsciously empowered purposeless failure. Are you guided by "animal-thoughts" or "human-thoughts?" Invisible thought processes control your behavior in the visible world. You are a **"thought-evolved-being."** Behavior is always a function of the brain. You may have two brain processes or neural systems competing with each other, or experiencing trauma/injury; resulting in pathological brain-circuitry diagnosed as **OCD** in one individual, and **PTSD** in another. Law-enforcement expectations blur the line when experiencing OCD and PTSD. What stage-presentations of self-exposed "bias," "expectations" and "beliefs" did you bring to the diagnostic evaluation; that may have infected your situational diagnosis, more than your actual in-the-moment behavioral display—self-modification of your self-presentation to the medical staff. Your "expert" conducting the diagnosis may have had a horrible day and never really fully-present doing your evaluation, resulting in a lifetime of side-effect heavy prescription meds. As long as they are legal! On bad-days, we can, with a clear-conscience; occasionally be "justified" to mix one of our legal-pills with legal-alcohol, for a more legal-medicated mood of self-righteousness! Arrest a few adult-marijuana-capitalist-consumers for possession (arrest and incarceration for their own protection), for another dose of self-righteousness. Observe thyself—will you like what you interpret?

Quantum scientific investigations, require measuring quantum-particle super-positions of value, that can only be "brought-into-existence," through "observation." This observation simultaneously triggers a distant-cousin quantum particle to measure in the opposite value—instantaneously. Politicians utilize manipulated-disguised "crime-statistics" when they are positive for their campaign, and deny the value of "crime-statistics" that are negative. Crime-statistics can be initially designed to never document negativities unfavorable for the intended or expected conclusions. Context and categories cleverly designed to look "unbiased and informationally-loaded," but, **disguise unfavorable categories** and context through omission of subject-matter, or censored disclosure. When "society" documents citizen-behavior as a crime; that specific-incident will have to have been "observed" or "measured" in some-manner into a "statistic." That documented statistic alters as fast as the internet, (pert-near-non-local)—national and inter-national statistical measurements of crime, that infect our personal mental-measurement safety-assessment. National statistical measurements of crime infect our personal local safety-assessment in another feed-back loop we ignore. Quantum non-locality can be described through basic human-behavior; mental and physical feed-back loops that operate so smoothly and efficiently, that we forget we are on a reality ride-of-our-own making! "Non-locality" sounds local-crazy or crazy-local. There are some excellent best-selling book and video-based introductions to quantum-stuff; that will make you reconsider your pre-programmed bias and limiting beliefs concerning basic physical and directed mental-effort involving human-police-citizen interaction. Police behavior and citizen behavior as **"emergent phenomenon,"** requiring a mind to use its mind to investigate its mind, to monitor its mind, to correct its mind, to motivate its mind, keep the mind and host body fed and watered, to efficiently interact with other minds, to not disassociate into more minds, to interpret its mind, to mind its own mind—business! A crime not documented, still occurred, but the system is coincidentally designed to unrecognize the undisclosed obviousness in damage to the community—if (for a hundred plus real reasons), the citizen can not or choose **not to make-a-report**. I wish we had the option back in my "old-days" involving obviously injured victims who decline to press charges; available now for police-officers to detain a suspect involved in a domestic dispute where victim injuries are verified, even if this person verbally states they do not intend to ever press charges. During multiple levels of Army law-enforcement, I did have more incidents where the more violent female-significant other, was allowed to remain in the residence that night. The Army mandated that male-soldiers were ordered to report to their barracks (CQ) Charge-of-Quarters for that evening, and be assigned a barracks room.

NEGATIVE ATTITUDES CREATE

NEGATIVE EXPECTATIONS

RETICULAR ACTIVATING SYSTEM (RAS). Your sensory modalities, at the most basic level, automatically incorporate your thought processes as part of your personal response to the situation you have responded to. Your response is further flavored by your **emotional arousal** at that moment, influenced by your pre-programmed unconscious judgmental motivational behavioral conditioning. Some experts identify your RAS as how, during a complicated emergency response on your part, your memory of the event is difficult to consciously analyze. Your RAS took charge and decreased the importance of most of your sensory awareness, your focus was elsewhere. The memories are there, they will just require some effort to recall. When law-enforcement responds to emotional incidents, we have to be "adaptable" to this particular incident with all its specific nuances and flow. Adaptive thinking "self-talk" requires an open-mind and the ability to admit your initial pre-planning prior to arriving at the scene, needs modification and quickly. Can you "self-talk" yourself and other responding officers into a more positive attitude. **Attitudes become personalities**. A feeling of defeat can contaminate those around us, and make our responses more negative and possibly violent. Negative attitudes create negative expectations, the opposite of the positive adaptation potential all law-enforcement should energize.

RECOGNIZING AND UNDERSTANDING

POSITION OF FIXATION

Recent advancements in understanding cognition thru neuroimaging techniques, stresses the importance of human "eye-movements" for a police-officers "visual-attention" skill. Some experts propose that you cannot understand "attention" without understanding "eye-movements." For a police-officer, incoming visual information is useless without cognitive and perceptual processing. Your cognitive processes guide your mind-directed gaze control thru visual information analysis, in a feedback loop influencing your cognitive processes. Eye fixation influences a police-officer overcoming "limits-to-attention" that may be more limited by human physical properties, or an unfocused improper attitude. Your personal **"position-of-fixation"** can make-or-break your attention skills when evaluating a complex scene that you have been dispatched to. Investigations into "position-of-fixation," have revealed that you can miss a lot of visual information, especially "changes," from fixating on an object, to focusing your eyes "saccade" movements on another object. Your unconscious preferences for where you focus your visual attention, will be drawn effortlessly to your fixation point. Are those unconscious preferences viable and really where you should be looking. Human eyesight is equipped with **two different visual streams**—both providing two vital functions for the police-officer making initial contact with novel outside-stimuli. One neuronal route will control recognizing and understanding—is consciously accessible. The other neuronal route operating out of our access and awareness, is for "doing-behavior."

CONSCIOUS AND UNCONSCIOUS

COGNITIVE INTERPRETATION

Scientists have further identified the "Chemistry-of-Cognition" using Positron-Emission Tomography (PET) and radioactive emitters. We can get meaningful information concerning internal natural chemical mediators, neuronal metabolism and modulation. This is why we need to be very careful when altering the body's neurochemical environment—which influences critical visual processing programs thru cognitive-pharmacological intervention. Your visual attention helps keep track of human "**attitude-objects**" circulating in your awareness zone. You do not just have personal unconscious tendencies, you have "culturally" 2indoctrinated unconscious tendencies. Approach and withdrawal behavior requires some form of "appraisal," which usually begins with an unconscious appraisal, before conscious cognitive appraisal. Visual attention skills ensure the police-officer recognizes "**emotional-faces**" approaching their position. Emotional faces are so evolutionarily important, both for the display face, and the interpreting individual, that face muscles directly connect bone to skin. Can you think of any other place in your body that muscles directly connect bone to skin? Emotional faces must have evolutionary and survival value. Police-officers and parents are bombarded with <u>fake-emotional faces</u> of deceptive intent—which, being unnatural, are usually easily determined or intuited as fake. This individual requires some conscious reflection to counteract **potential deception;** conscious cognitive interpretation and decision-making inner-research is needed. Unconscious judgments continue while you consciously reflect—which process is making your decisions for you? Describe the last time you experienced an influential **unconscious judgment**. If you were aware of the unconscious-judgement as it occurred, that does not count. What was your personal "meaning" behind the judgment, and what did your unconscious judgment "mean" for citizen-police interaction.

<u>MIRROR-NEURON INFLUENCE</u>

Faces alone, are not sufficient information- <u>wise</u>, to make reliable "appraisals." Bias, racism and discrimination usually begin initially with facial recognition at the unconscious level. Facial characteristics have been proven to negatively influence the "blind-justice" expected of jurors—possibly creating unconscious-based guilty verdicts. Facial characteristics that provide such "thin-slices" of information about the person. Dr. Bargh warns us that it is better to have "seen the other person in action," before you trust your initial gut reaction to the same person. How sure are you that unconsciously, you do not "mimic" the other in your life right now. Scientists report that we are born with this innate-tendency to mimic. If you no longer unconsciously mimic the good and the bad of the people you interact with, when did you recognize this counterproductive unconscious mimicking. When did you counteract this genetic programming and how? Clinical investigation has proven that just because we are actually "doing-mimicry," does not mean that a different part of your brain that "knows," understands that you are "doing-mimicry," actually succeeded in bringing such information to conscious awareness. My second book, Policing Private personalities, includes human-mirror-neuron phenomena including imitation, mimicry and mirroring. I believe all police-officers should have a class on the implications of the human-mirror-neuron system—especially the influence on police-citizen interaction. Police-citizen interaction influences each other—behaviorally. Every police-officer should have total understanding of all external **influences on their behavior**, especially if internal mirror-neuronal influence is allowing this external influence—out of our awareness.

UNCONSCIOUS MIRRORING

INTERNET DIGITAL INFECTION

Unconscious behavior suggestions from outside stimuli, can be received and acted upon—without your awareness. Trying to quit unwanted behavior, like addictions, unfortunately activate the same neuronal-craving pathways. Try reminding yourself that you intend quitting what you crave without using the same neuronal pathways that got you addicted in the first place. Unconscious mirroring is also occurring when you are on social-media, out of your awareness, becoming **digitally-contagious**. Dr. Bargh described this digitally-contagious process as allowing digitally-presented people that you don't even know, to "digitally-infect" you to the point that you either "digitally-infect" someone else, or you physically-infect in person. It is hard to properly investigate "social-setting" in relation to mental challenges and threats, when you are safely at home in a chair, while being digitally infected by someone you do not know properly through honest interaction. Do you really want to "fit-in," or are you "pretending" you want to fit-in—imitation, mimicry and mirroring unconsciously or consciously. You behave differently with people you will never really meet, especially if you are confident, you will never-ever meet them, or will never seriously try. You are not conscious or aware of all the "**effects**" you have on others and they have on you. Self-awareness skills also include recognizing environmental potentiation out-of-your control— "thinking-planning-behavior modification." Will all your pre-programmed unconscious motor-programming (self-initiated responses) automatically get you to a place of safety? Will you have to rely instead, on all your pre-programmed unconscious motor-programming skills involving weapon-use? <u>Human-perception means active participation</u> influencing our internal neural representations—that is how we are designed, especially with law-enforcement duties. Human perception is distorted by attention, your attentional state. Dr. Schwartz stresses that we all can, "**think ourselves into a new brain.**"

Unconscious thinking about a certain subject out of your awareness, utilizes the same area of the brain that conscious thoughts about the same subject, occur. Humans evolved to unconsciously just like someone more when they first meet, if that person appears to behave more like us. Police-officers at the scene of a complicated crime scene, need to easily, effectively and correctly determine "what predicts what?" Most crime scenes do not provide patterns and sequences that immediately provide all the objective measurements and reliable data necessary to solve this crime—requiring some initial "gut-reactions" to develop an investigative plan and provide guidance. Your gut (usually) propels your motivational behavioral in the right direction; your personal **"mechanics-of-intuition,"** until conscious cognitive skills identify the proper steps to document and solve the crime you responded to. What unconscious "filters" prevent you from seeing reality as it really is? Have your "negative" **unconscious filters** increased their control over your behavior more, since you joined law-enforcement? It happens to most of us. Are your most energized unconscious filters triggered by normal routine "cues in your environment?" Random unconscious counterproductive filters instead of cognitively inspired productive conscious filtering.

INTENTIONAL CONSCIOUS CONTROL

Police-officers, who, interacting with external stimuli (situational context), seem to lose "independent control" of their behavior, have given control to the same external stimuli. You are no longer in charge. External stimuli have offered you emotional and behavioral suggestions that uncharacteristically modifies your behavior—unconscious imitation. Rookies are "community-oriented" and are going to make a positive difference—then reality slaps us in the face as we become veterans. We begin to patrol from the position of **"power,"** with less and less community intent. Science has proven that "community-oriented" police-officers are less racist! Did any "police-trainer" instruct you on approach/avoidance issues directly, or was it inferred in various training situations? Approach-avoidance-withdrawal behavioral responses, is real verified science—almost a field in itself. We **approach and avoid,** usually behaviorally motivated instantly from the unconscious, preferring or falsely believing that it was a conscious decision. Not simple "priming" from a previous dispatch! While on patrol, you always have a subconsciously-functioning internal partner operating out of your conscious awareness, that is similar to your conscious self. The similarities have different goals and objectives, usually "ghost-thoughts" ambiguously partially almost recognized, some critical for successful police-citizen interaction. Regaining control of your uninhibited unconscious impulses and behavior begins by taking intentional conscious control of your **behavioral intentions**—which, obviously every police-officer should have.

BEHAVIORAL ATTENTION

SACRED CONSCIOUS CONTROL

Symbolism, metaphor, schemas in relation to movement, and unconscious contextual categorical representation; are your "imaginative structures in understanding," Although they were originally devised to assist you, these mental-strengths now stand between you and true conscious understanding of reality, your environment. While your behavioral intentions are processed in one part of the brain, another part of your brain controls the "guiding" of what you behaviorally intended. Behaviors you "intend" to perform require a separate brain process to guide the behavior. When I investigated murders, we did not have "crime-scene processing teams." We, the responding investigator had to do everything. A few times, with non-stop interruptions, complicated murder scenes, short-staffed, other police-actions seeking my attention, backed up interviews and interrogations; I felt a little cloudy in my thinking—reaching the limits of my patience and cognitive abilities. It may have been caused by two distinct areas of my brain seeking my behavioral attention, the sacred conscious-control—with different evolutionarily designed instructional programs trying to help me along. Neuronally, we have one program "thinking", while another program is responsible for behavioral-expression. You will always be responsible for the "**future-consequences**" of your behavioral choices and expression.

It is extremely difficult to verify for yourself, law-enforcement "suppositions" and "paradigms" that you merely inherited and subconsciously stored as truth-memories, from your instructors, trainers, supervisors, friends, strangers, family, and religion. Suppositions and Paradigms influence and determine who you arrest, who you show compassion and discretionary policing for, and who you end up shooting? They convince you that certain areas and certain people need your presence, whether it is actually beneficial and positive or not. Are we so busy, and preoccupied in certain neighborhoods to keep "enforcement" out of richer neighborhoods by design or accident? Suppositions and paradigms are everything in law-enforcement. It is how we keep a clear conscious while reviewing our mandatory police-actions taken earlier. From Policing Private Personalities, Sam Luckey

Some evolutionary biologists identify how readily modern humans lie and deceive each other as an indication that human readiness to easily **lie and deceive**—might have a genetic (impression-management) basis. **Self-deception** is a real issue. If modern humans continue to lie and deceive because it increases mating selection advantages, then we may be producing more skillful liars and deceivers, further contaminating our gene pool negatively. Sometimes we feel justified to convince others to see ourselves as we see ourselves, even if it requires multiple small-lies. Some experts describe that without a small amount of untruthfulness, social-interaction would get messier and more complicated. What would an Implicit Association Test reveal about how your past experience influence on the quality of all your attitude association social interactions? **Hidden biases** out of your awareness, may hinder your capability to recognize "signaling discriminatory behavior," in yourself and others. Simple social-behaviors like speech discomfort indicators, may not be recognized if you are biased enough.

"Don't take anything personally. You can see how important this agreement is. Taking nothing personally helps you break many habits and routines that trap you in the dream of hell and cause needless suffering. Just by practicing this agreement you begin to break dozens of teeny, tiny agreements that cause you to suffer." From **THE FOUR AGREEMENTS**, Don Miguel Ruiz.

"When you are on the scene of a crime and spend your conscious energies visiting and trapped in past transgressions and insults, you may very well miss a knife or other object headed your way." From *POLICING PRIVATE PERSONALITIES*, Sam Luckey

SUBCONSCIOUSLY PREPARING FOR FUTURE STATES

Interpretation of meaning triggers unconscious and conscious expectation mental imagery—propelling your behavior in the right direction—we hope. Experts remind us of the importance in understanding that your thoughts differ from meaning. Thoughts in your mind can identify external patterns that reveal structure or a "set-of-relations" interpreted as **meaning.** We can then alert other police-officers of the "meaning" we detected, so they can activate thoughts in their mind, encouraging them to identify external patterns in their environment that reveal structure, importance etc. Behaviorally, (consciously or unconsciously) **preparing for "future-states,"** requires goals and motivation, in what Dr. Bargh calls "the third time zone of the hidden-mind." Name the last ten unconscious influences you detected. Unconscious motivational forces may be preparing you for the wrong "future!" Not good for law-enforcement. Preparing for "future-states" is made much easier if you really understand your unconscious motivations, intentions and lies—no longer ignoring and covering-up self-deception. Baruch Spinoza warned us that we are, "ignorant of the causes by which we are desired to desire anything." While we are skilled to prepare for "future-states," we are less skilled or cognizant of how our more powerful unconscious drags **emotional turmoil from the recent**

90

past—into our less powerful conscious mental programming. You will usually be feeling a certain way—long before you tie it to what just happened "at-you," just a moment ago—unconscious mental issues have caught you, not the other way around.

"We're bombarded by huge amounts of information, and its coming into our body and we're processing it. It's coming in through our sense organs, and percolating up and up, and at each step we're eliminating information and finally, what is bubbling up to consciousness is the one that's most self-serving." **Candace Pert Ph.D.**

PRE-JUDGMENT MOTIVATION

Can you recognize the difference between consciously motivated reflective thoughts, from automatic thoughts birthed from your implicit knowledge—out-of-your awareness? **We patrol in dissonance, with contradictory navigational devices** like motivated impulses, intuitions and reason, that rarely agree or translate into the same behavioral modification. Mental harmony is rare. Police-citizen interaction involves group pre-formed mental images of default attributes, heavily influenced out of your awareness, influencing all your behavioral options. This-group, that-group, us and them, like-us—not like-us, in-group favoritism triggers. You begin your police-citizen interaction with fixed mental categorization pictures of the "group" or groups you have automatically assigned the person you are facing. Routine unverified prejudgment default characteristics as motivator for our behavioral options. Some experts report that "**stereotyping**," not from a racist point-of-view, has benefits for initiating **quick assessments** of six or more distinct category identifiers; that assist in narrowing down the individual into a "distinctive-individual." Culturally influenced stereotyping, as practiced by undisciplined and deceiving humans, has more negative consequences, even violent and deadly consequences. You do not need to be emotionally disturbed to stereotype; you may not feel any discomfort at all. It is not uncommon for people to automatically negatively stereotype their own race; illogically maintaining social disadvantages, out-group homogeneity effect and hidden discrimination intention. We lazily "favor-the-familiar" as a mental attribute. Mahzarin R. Banaji and Anthony G. Greenwald, in their book BLIND SPOT: Hidden Biases of Good People, highlight: "Attitudes have both reflective and automatic forms." "People are often unaware of disagreement between the reflective and automatic forms of their own attitudes and stereotypes." "Explicit bias is infrequent; implicit bias is pervasive." "Implicit race attitudes (automatic race preferences) contribute to discrimination against Black Americans."

Preparing for future states—includes raid-planning. For 15 years I lectured about/against the War on Drugs and the prohibition of marijuana for a huge basic criminology course at Indiana University in Bloomington twice a year. (Back in the Army, while at DEA school, I openly protested the prohibition of marijuana.) This did not do any good as the Army had me work stateside and overseas on drug operations for years. When I was reassigned stateside and was told I would once again be a CID Team Chief for the Drug Suppression Team—contributed to my decision to get out of the Army. During this time, I lectured for five years about the Branch Davidian/WACO raid and the Ruby Ridge tragedy. I stress—it has been proven that self-doubt is not bad. When the supervisor of the Branch Davidian ATF disaster changed a night-time surprise no-knock raid, into a day-time surprise no-knock—I wonder did he entertain any self-doubt about the obvious stupidity of turning it into a day-time raid. What expectations did he hold that "primed" his conscious and unconscious thought processes to expect success? All the planning up to that point had been based on a night-time raid. All the ATF agents as they approached, I am sure they had self-doubt, but were not allowed to act on it. I am also convinced that the raid-supervisor knew that a postal-carrier had

92

accidentally tipped off the Branch Davidians. What really upset me the most was that if the local Sheriff had just called David Koresh to the Sheriff's office a few days earlier, David Koresh always complied. He always came in when asked. We would have had the leader detained and the "sheep" would have more easily complied. For five years I ended all my lectures on the Branch Davidians by charging that the only reason the ATF wanted a big-televised raid, instead of a quiet arrest by the Sheriff out of camera view, was they wanted publicity. Their blood-line, their budget was all that mattered. The life-force of their agency was about to be slashed. At Ruby-Ridge I don't see how the FBI sniper can live with himself, shooting the suspects wife while holding a baby. Unconscious belief systems infecting our government. With fully functioning free-will, government agents released control of their behavior to bureaucrats—whose motives were financially dominated.

REWARDS THAT BEHAVIORALLY MOTIVATE

Neuroscientists have proven that you do not have to be consciously aware that your "**mental-reward-centers**" have determined (for you?) that you received what you "subconsciously-perceived" to be a reward from outside sources. Internal unconscious mute congratulations maybe, out of your awareness. You may even feel more positive and satisfied at that moment, but you just don't know why. Police-officers experience various "**rewards**" during their shifts. Rewards that are unconsciously and consciously recognized, but are not universal from officer to officer. If I did not get a complicated dispatch right before end-of-shift, I took that as a "reward." Catching some felon personal to my thought processes, can be a reward. I took extra time to review "wanted-posters" before my shifts. I wonder if my "mental-reward" processes determined my "**hunt**" for the "wanted;" from the law-enforcement mission side, or ancient evolutionary "hunting" thought processes. Dr. Bargh reminds us that "pursuit" or hunting for a suspect, "**patterns your thoughts**, mental images and even dreams in entirely unintended ways." Law-enforcement are extremely susceptible to improper behavior, when on an emotionally-charged "hunt;" you will unconsciously make-decisions/choices and prefer to work alongside other law-enforcement officers who are behaviorally charged-up and motivated as you are—probably willing to ignore any **in-the-streets—judgment** and punishment. The wanted person may have not been physically present when I began the "hunt," but, was "psychologically" present in my mind! Rewards that motivate you consciously and unconsciously.

SELF-DOUBT IS VERY NORMAL

Your unconscious is empowered to more successfully **decline temptations** from an advance, mentally intended pre-temptation point-of-view—than conscious will-power empowers at the time of the temptation. You just aren't tempted that much as you make contact with desired temptation. Conscious will-power includes fluctuating intent **"justification" issues**. As Dr. Bargh describes, if you want to eat less junk food and drink less alcohol, don't bring it home to begin with—self-control abilities are not static—they can be modified and improved in advance. Taking control of your life— requires giving your unconscious some concrete instructions and guidance. Somehow, we are evolutionarily programmed in a way that self-control-abilities operate more successfully from your unconscious point-of-view. Did the Behaviorists, know this? It is time for you to brainstorm some ideas designed by you, for you, concerning defined and specific/concrete goals and objectives your unconscious can "make-it-so!" Dr. Bargh describes that "**effective self-controllers set up their environment**" for success. Unfortunately, this is not possible for law-enforcement. We just have to be well-trained, disciplined, properly supplied (and a miracle occurs) and good co-workers; because we may think of our patrol-area as "our-environment," but it is not. Unconscious beneficial behavior, intended—sounds Sci-Fi to me! I understand unquestioned (wrong) assumptions and unconscious habitual behaviors energizing their negative influence, but unconscious programming self-neural-plasticity for successful police-citizen interaction, especially de-escalation techniques, seem the proper direction. Thank-you Dr. Bargh. Police-officers have a job where it is easy to graduate from a loving "rookie" to one who sees law-enforcement from an us and them point-of-view. When your unconscious processing skills have been biased into full compliance, (justified?) divisive ways to see and interact behaviorally—with our world as we see that world—not the way it really is. Police-officers do not work in isolation. <u>Self-doubt is very normal</u>, do not be alarmed.

SOCIAL CREATURES AND ENERGIZED BEHAVIOR

Unconscious social-needs motivate your behavior, probably more than conscious intended (recognized) social-needs, as we are social-creatures. Our "reward-centers," for most of us, encourage "helping-others," but, science has proven that most of us will help only if we are not in a hurry. Simple as that! Counter-productive and immature **unconscious goals and needs** has been proven to energize behavior that **"tunes-your-attention"** to any information that is relevant to your immature and counter-productive unconscious goals and needs. Information that counters your unconscious intentions in life, will be unconsciously determined "irrelevant." You will find "justification" for ignoring someone in need—**unconscious negative values**. It takes less than a second for you to be (slimed) subliminally and behaviorally "choice" altered. Your memories will be recalled into awareness, biased by unconscious goals and needs so deeply, that your memory will seem normal even though it was altered and changed from reality. Clinical investigations have found that almost half of your thoughts—have nothing to do with what you are actually "doing." Dr. Bargh describes that when we catch our mind "wandering," you really <u>just caught up to where your unconscious took you</u>. Improper and immature unconscious goals and objectives that you do not know you have, will override any "long-term values and beliefs," unfortunately even "moral-beliefs" will be pushed aside. Not good for law-enforcement. Meet your director, the unconscious.

We also dream our undisciplined and counterproductive needs, desires, goals and objectives, sometimes confusing us in the morning. The "problems" you take to bed with you, will utilize the same brain processing centers to solve those problems while you sleep, as you utilized while awake. Your unconscious keeps you awake because your problems require specific-concrete plans, and your unconscious is better at more ambiguous potential-solving future goal-related ambitions, if you fail to give concise problem-solving needs. While you sleep, your unconscious (uncontrolled intrusive thoughts) may be trying to solve incomplete poorly-defined goals and problems from your entire lifetime. Problems and goals you have not consciously energized or intended solving strategies in years, if not decades—no need for solving these old "goals and problems." Your unconscious still remembers them and treats them as active goals and problems. Experts remind us that your unconscious, 24 hours a day, is also examining your environment in its effort to solve your goals and problems, even if they do not exist anymore. Dr. Bargh asks us to recognize if our internal-**self talk** is leading to more **"self-control" and "self-regulation,"** or leading us to undisciplined thought processes. Temporary goals and problems can take control of your unconscious as much as the big-long-term life issues. How much "free-will" can you really possess, if you have no self-control or self-regulation skills?

EFFECTIVE UNCONSCIOUS POWERS

Dr. Bargh promotes that your use of unconscious powers properly intended, will be the most "effective," and he means more effective than conscious effort. To increase the effectiveness of your unconscious powers, to improve police-citizen interaction—you must take control of your conscious thoughts—now! Develop your plan now. Determine **tactical-short-term** potentiality and combine them with **long-term** strategy—this will help your unconscious become more content and cooperative with the conscious. Have you ever intentionally created a good habit on your own, since childhood—with parental or caretaker guidance? Recognize that hidden influences, are not just "out-there" in your environment. Hidden influences are also floating around in your unconscious and conscious. Do you have to internally "talk" yourself into self-control, or do you only need to think it? Where is the dividing line between **"talking" to yourself and only "thinking,"** when facing environmental interaction cues and needs—especially police-citizen interaction desired de-escalation behavior. Do you hear voices, or is this all-neuronal simulation stimulation.

ENVIRONMENTAL INTERACTION

Control over your behavior occurs in a different brain area, when environmental stimulus switches you from "internal-thought" processes, to thought-processes evolutionarily designed for environmental interaction behavioral success. Your **inner-thoughts** (alone) are generated by one brain area, and **environmental interaction** goal and activity requires another. Do you see this as more ways for something to go wrong, or see this team action as synergistically improving success? Environmental interaction is the name of the game for law-enforcement. Get it right—or get out! How easily do you determine when your "unconscious impulses and influences" are not helping with police-citizen interaction. If you have no faith in your own "goals and objectives", obviously, chances of success will be self-defeated from the beginning. Will you need a "team-effort? If your plan will not succeed because of timing issues or insufficient supply/personnel issues; modify your goals to more manageable less-stressful "implementation-intentions." We are bombarded with Sci-Fi movies about "mind-control," not so much about personal unconscious and conscious issues.

PARTICIPANT IMPLEMENTATION CONDITION

The book "BEFORE YOU KNOW IT", by Dr. John Bargh, I recommend for law-enforcement—it will help you with Police-Citizen interaction—and your unconscious and conscious mental processes. Dr. Bargh details a clinical investigation involving "**implementation intentions and effective goal pursuits**" by researchers P. M. Gollwitzer and V. Brandstatter. The following is an actual quote from Dr. Bargh's book: This study included clinically investigating mental racial overtones in shootings among our citizenry. "White participants were more likely to **mistakenly shoot** an unarmed black person than unarmed white persons." Just as alarming it was revealed that, "and less likely to correctly identify an armed white than an armed black person." The investigation had an alternate method intended, a "implementation intention condition" that required participants to tell themselves "If I see a person, then I will ignore his race!" "Bias was significantly reduced." Dr. Bargh added, "The implications here for law-enforcement are obvious." I did not have these modern neuroscientific investigations to learn from back in the "old-days," when I was in law-enforcement. All we had was Freud and Jung on one side, and armies of behaviorists who did not believe investigating mind and consciousness issues was worthwhile—or even possible. Then came the computer age. Did your law-enforcement academy mention this study that clearly documented racist influences in shootings?

NEURON/SYNAPTIC SIMULATION STIMULATION

Do your "compulsions" influence unconscious weapon-use preparation? Are you a well-trained police-robot who does not need to actively-process incoming sensory-stimuli as part of your attentional-processing skills? Your mind influences (default-awareness) which neurotransmitters are released, further influencing your potential courses-of-action; especially which **"associated-probabilities"** influence your behavioral options. Which novel problem-solving ideas never even enter your awareness? What negative intentions do you unconsciously cultivate and empower? **Neurotransmitters** keep your thoughts, the positive and the negative, empowered to have strong behavioral influence until you change those same thoughts. If all your possibilities and potentialities are pre-determined, limiting your unconscious-mind/brain processes options and choices, then do you really have volitional freedom-of-choice? Sometimes our own internally generated **simulation-stimulation** thought-processes, empower more habitual undisciplined pre-programmed neural-circuitry behavioral responses, than the actual external stimuli we responded to. Willful volitional choices concerning what we habitually intend attention and focus-on, should not be under outside control.

Neuronally based marketing schemes and advertisements only need less than a second to alter your brain-chemistry—especially consumers with undisciplined distracted attention skills! During a routine-patrol, how many "less-than-a-second" subliminal messages enter our unconscious and conscious mental processing. If you are not aware enough, you won't recognize all this outside influence on your inner-turmoil. Not just our children are vulnerable to **scientifically crafted mass-marketing**. Adults who "adult-toy" themselves into financial ruin, need to remember that when you shop "hungry," you buy more of everything, not just food/beverage items. Dr. Bargh warns us that our unconscious is so powerful, when compared to the conscious, that it is your unconscious that is probably determining your goals in life; if they are being met—and especially, how you feel about that. What Dr. Bargh calls your unconscious "default mode of operation." People unpleasant to be around, interact from their **unconscious "default mode of**

operation." Your unconscious may be more creative than your conscious mind? You can positively program your unconscious to conduct more positive insightful helpful mental-processing. Out of your awareness, your unconscious hopefully has actual intended positive goals, objectives and guidance providing "novel-solutions." It has been proven that the same brain processes that realize and analyze "problems," also are the same brain processes that unconsciously problem solve for you, sometimes against you if you have pre-programmed your unconscious with garbage.

SACCADE VISUAL PURSUIT MOVEMENTS

Your visual fixation point is assisted thru "saccade" rapid eye movements that keep your eyes on moving targets, usually without conscious intention. We also use saccade "pursuit movements" which allow us to match movement velocity—visual-cognitive activity. Your "**position-of-fixation**" also influences visual-memory. Scientists use eye-tracking as a form of behavioral methodology for cognitive scientist to utilize. Police use both temporal phase functions, fixation of gaze and saccadic eye movement. Computers allow modern scientist to prove that during your natural "saccade" eye movement, they can sneak objects into your visual field, and move other items around, and you do not notice. Fixation seems to be the only way to keep saccade eye movements from interfering with your visual search analysis. Scientists have proven that without **fixation-of-gaze**, "saccadic suppression" during natural saccadic eye-movement occurs, and any pertinent visual-information will not be processed. You don't just have to have fixation; the duration of fixation is just as important. There is potential that just during a complex emotional event, your natural saccadic eye-movement may prevent you from recognizing danger. Perhaps, a citizen properly trained, could pull a firearm out and you may have missed the "change" in your environment, merely because of natural saccadic eye-movement. Sometimes **your mind fills in these visual and auditory gaps** with the wrong information. Natural vision neuroanatomical structures and optical properties may only make you think you observed a gun—initial-visual-computation. Novel visual stimuli usually takes control of your "position-of-fixation." When we see a face, most of our "facial-recognition" skills devote 90% of your visual fixation on the nose, mouth and eyes.

Unmediated sensory awareness allows your action-behavior to become pure awareness-experience. **Self-control** with purpose is more automatic without conscious interference. Arousal control is the first step in regaining "focus" intention and attention. "Anxiety" is considered a "rehearsal of fear." A little anxiety is expected, but excessive anxiety can be lowered through breathing exercises while self-analysis identifies why. The internet provides free "stress-management" ideas and examples. Anxiety may reach the level of "**negative-thoughts**" that suppresses your normal "frontal-lobe" mental processing. This means that anxiety may limit your ability for normal "constructive-discourse." De-escalation does not even enter your mind and may never be considered as an available primary option. A balanced point-of-view is replaced by unplanned and unwelcome miss-statements and simplified and rushed solutions. Perspective analysis -vs- time restraints energized by personal judgmental mental architecture and your attitude at that moment. Attitudes become personalities. Your behavior reveals your personalities of the moment. Experts remind us that their "personality-profiles" are not intended to be utilized as "predictors of behavior," which, I have to admit confuses me. If an applicant says that he was not hired because he failed a "personality-profile," that raises "questions." "Screening-out" potentially negative applicants are not the intent of "personality-profiles."

CHAPTER THREE

<u>PATTERNS WITHIN PATTERNS</u>

<u>RELATIONS WITHIN RELATIONS</u>

The emotional addictions that you carry and unconsciously empower, can usually be traced back to basic "belief structures" that may have their origin from your childhood. When you project your beliefs and "sense-of-self" upon the world, and you don't like what comes back at you, awaken to intentional intended change. Self-directed neural-plasticity is a skill that can be self-improved—with or without self-help books. Don't wait until the world forces you to comply. "**Addictive behaviors,**" are not only drug-related. Humans have the innate ability to not just experience an event, but can see the experience from a "whole" experience point-of-view. Experiences create "expectations" that you may not really want to energize and store. You have evolved to easily detect "**patterns**" (assumptions) in others usually pretty efficiently, while most of us ignore the internal "patterns" of behavior that continuously entrap us in habits of negativity and self-pity. Critical thinking or reviewing our own behavior—is not criticism. You can intend and motivate "detachment" without negative consequences. Patterns of behavior influenced by your experience in law-enforcement, include <u>unconscious auto-detection skills</u> involved with pattern recognition, indicating your presence is needed in the community. Observing citizens involved in normal routine community relationships are unconsciously analyzed, until a questionable "relationship" becomes "conscious" worthy. We recognize, analyze and initiate behavior based on detecting "**patterns-within-patterns,**" similar to syntax. We determine "**relations-within-relations**" as easily as we recognize "metaphors." The old sketchy "physiological psychology" classes have become cognitive neuroscience—that I enjoy and trust. I like Dr. Shermer's description of neurons as, "complex electrochemical information-processing machines." "Most" neurons function as "excitatory," or "inhibitory," operating in a "on or off, all or nothing" system.

Neuroscientists have identified the chemical-transmitter "**dopamine**," as the "Belief-Drug." Your associative-learning skills, coupled with your interpretation of rewards (reward-system), depends on dopamine operant conditioning—behavior reinforcer mental processes. Like reward, repeat behavior! Your brain stem has neurons that produce dopamine, the location of which stresses how important evolutionarily, dopamine was for human development. Your "sensation-of-pleasure" takes many forms, including **interpretation of rewards**. Police-citizen interaction with someone struggling with addictions, can be related to their dopamine system. Your personal struggles with your dopamine system can be tempered by determining if your dopamine system activates only for pleasure/rewards; or does it reflect your "motivational" need/wants/desires. Does "pleasure" require activation as motivation? Some experts identify "**not-getting-the-reward**" as motivational-anxiety, especially if your belief-system motivates a "reward-is-justified" and I will get my reward, no matter what! Especially with drug-addictions. Is the behavior that your dopamine system rewards, behavior you are proud of? Dopamine fluctuation influences police-officers' skills at detecting meaning and patterns involving outside stimuli. Dopamine levels influence your creative problem-solving de-escalation success or failures. Excess dopamine may create habits-of-thought, imaginary patterns and meanings not actually present, "problems in patternicity."

PATTERN SEEKING DOPAMINE

Police-officers patrolling in a community-of-noise, seek out patterns and meanings in order to avoid "false-negatives" that can get you embarrassed, injured or killed. How many different "self-fulfilling prophecies" do you energize every shift? Does your dopamine system influence specific clearly **"goal-defined"** thinking in a good way? Or, is your dopamine system out-of-balance because you are so overly mentally stimulated and stressed, eat the wrong foods, and have no clear goals and objectives in life? Dopamine may be the biggest factor in your success or failures at **pattern-seeking** creative genius. Visual cortex activation and excess dopamine can take you on a wild-wild ride. Whatever environmental outside-stimuli fragments reach your awareness, your mind will always try to make sense and find **real or imagined** "coherence." Even in error, you will dopamine-belief yourself into behavior that just seems right—even if you were very wrong and the auto-behavior auto-emotion made matters much worse! Beliefs develop before self-justification summarizations arise. Your beliefs netted behavior before verification.

What unverified beliefs do you enthusiastically pass on to others? See beliefs that you transmit into others as actual "objects in physical space." If the receiver does not actually challenge your transmitted belief with "skeptic-based" rejection mental processes; just simply understanding your description of the belief as spoken to you; requires a **secondary process of rejection** to prevent the false belief from taking root in your mind. Otherwise, this "belief" neural-activity becomes part of your unconscious belief system, influencing out of your awareness, all your police-citizen interaction feelings-of-conviction and self-righteousness. How many of your **"negative-expectations"** are really just unconsciously empowered, unverified beliefs, inserted inappropriately into your police-citizen interaction. Do we pre-judge everybody influenced by false-belief negative expectations? The power of your mind is clearly portrayed when your cortex can be electrically stimulated to produce false "beliefs" that you are experiencing an "out-of-body" experience. While "floating" above your body—you will believe and passionately defend your belief—that you were floating. You'd scream take a picture, and not believe that same picture when it shows no floating alternate you!

DETECTING INTENTIONAL STRUCTURES

Police-officers and archaeologists understand the old saying: "Absence of evidence—is not evidence of absence." We know suspicious "stuff" is going on in our community—out of our awareness. At this point, does your imagination assist in your search for meaning detection, or does it just distract you from here/now presence—in the moment, especially concerning "features not yet observed"? Deep in your own mind, can you detect a difference between patrolling with **imagination**, or patrolling with **intuition**? Do you project interpretations of truth that are really hindsight bias, confirmation bias and all the other "cognitive-biases"? You have multiple sensory modalities—are your **"predictive-theories"** constructing "meaning" intuitively or imaginatively? Is there "intentional structure" in the meaning you have detected? Did your thought processes and intentions express correctly what you ended up actually "expressing?" Frustration, fear, anger and even anxiety as repetitive associations, can interfere with verbal expression as much as behavioral expression— especially when projecting your reinterpreted cognitive dysfunction back at citizenry. Warranted or not, a police-officer displaying **poor verbal skills**, decreases chances at de-escalation successes—relying more on brute force, anger, firearms, unconscious habits and reflexes—that may have no positive influences at all for this particular situation. Your competence with <u>communication feed-back analysis language-skills</u>—may become a biased, impulsive or self-pity impotent mood—counter-productive for law-enforcement.

BELIEFS AS SOCIAL PARADIGM INDOCTRINATION

You entered law-enforcement heavily influenced by "<u>motivated-social-cognition</u>," unaware of its influence, especially during "<u>hierarchal social interactions</u>," belief-filtering your ego-behavior, with "belief-confirmations," real or imagined! Conflicting incoming data may trigger an emotional auto-reaction from your learned-emotional response library, confirmed "appropriate" thru **after-the-fact rationalization**, slimed in self-righteous attribution bias. Long-term well-meaning police-community team-effort programs that really do not work, seem to be dragged-on because we have already put so much time, tax-dollars and effort into the program, "sunk-cost bias!" How much bias and racism, the "framing-effect," weighed down by police- "anchoring-bias," influences your departments "status-quo-bias." Uncertainty is not just a personal issue; it infects entire departments. Michael Shermer, in his book The Believing Brain, highlights 25 "bias" issues infecting modern humans. He describes that humans are experts at calling-out "others" for their contradictory data bias issues, while ignorant of their own—unaware of the basic implicit sequence learning that got them into conflict, real or imagined. How well defined are your "intuitive-morals?" Your beliefs and social-paradigm indoctrinations, will drive your perceptual analysis confidence, more than the actual incident you were dispatched to. Does your convergence-of-evidence mental model reaffirm and "agree-with-observation?" Self-deception and illusion infect the best of us! Your thoughts infect the present moment!

Unconscious recognition is usually easier to alert your conscious detection skills that something needs your attention, while contextual and category "recall," is more difficult to achieve cognitive success. Symbolic information and **meaningless patterns** can attract and keep your attention because we are evolutionarily designed to find novel solutions and keep analyzing and analyzing any input. For a police-officer it is also important to have attention skills that allow breaking contact at some point in your pattern detection—especially thought processes. How behaviorally hooked are you on "local cultural templates" that frame the way you think about and see the world? How behaviorally hooked are you on "criminology cultural templates" that frame the way you patrol, think and see your community? When you communicate during police-citizen interaction, all your past (memory-stored) experience customizes speaking sequences for you, automatically. Your cultural communication templates compete with your police cultural communication templates. Then your **(belief-systems)** bias, prejudice, and racial communication templates sneak in. Your internal model of self-censorship, unconsciously analyzing the future consequences of current communication you direct at others; balancing helpful advantageous police-speak—while understanding your behavioral consequences in the present and in the future.

PSYCHOLOGICAL CONSTRUCTS—WISDOM AND BELIEFS

We would like to pass on our accumulated "wisdom" beliefs to our children, and even rookies we train. Yet, a universal definition of wisdom is pretty elusive. A 1990 edited book on Wisdom, contained 13 different definitions of wisdom. "Measuring" wisdom is as elusive (external validation/verification) as verifying all your unconscious "beliefs" are based in reality. Wisdom and beliefs influence your police-citizen interaction success-rates. Experts Susan Bluck and Judith Gluck stress five important aspects essential for wisdom— "cognitive ability, insight, reflective attitude, concern for others, and real-world skills." All five aspects are clearly aligned with law-enforcement citizen-interaction, especially **concern for others and insight.** They also recommend that a three-fold analysis for "wisdom" include interpersonal, society and intrapersonal aspects. For law-enforcement, wisdom includes recognizing your **"uncertainty"** in specific police-skills and understanding the real-meaning behind just what you responded to. Theories of Wisdom include implicit and explicit aspects as "psychological constructs." "Stress is a form of anxiety." Deepak Chopra. Anxiety is a rehearsal of fear. Challenges to personal "belief-structures" are challenges to our very personal specialness and exaggerated qualities considered "wisdom." Developmental psychiatry investigator, Michael Shermer, has convinced me that our beliefs, counterintuitively; really are mentally accepted and stored as fact, before we understand their truthiness, or why we accept the belief as fact. Dr. Shermer calls this shaky belief-system-of-beliefs, **"belief-dependent-realism."**

Sensory-perception input, mentally cross-referenced neural-imaging is useless, if you do not have memory—association skills—comparative identification/meaning threat-assessments developed in a timely efficient manner. You have the **"reality" of the situation** you responded to as it really is, competing inside your head, neuronally modified by your very personal ideation and expectations from reality. This means that your idea of reality thru selective memory, ambiguously fluctuates, reflecting your at-that-moment unconscious library of beliefs, expectations and judgments. Do you recognize when your learned action-behavior is being modified, dependent on your realistic and unrealistic beliefs? Truly understanding your reality, may reveal clashes and inconsistencies involving your beliefs. Police act as **"diagnostic-belief-engines,"** as we investigate and interpret what evidence and witness statements disclose. On-the-scene police-initiated summaries often reflect more about the police-officer speaking (projecting), than the actual crime-scene. Stanford psychologist David Rosenhan, conducted some very clever investigations concerning mental facilities and their accuracy involving the diagnosis of insane or sane. We hold the "belief" that this should be an easy diagnosis, especially when well-trained and experienced mental-health experts are the ones deciding sane or insane status. The evaluators **"beliefs" swayed diagnosis** more than it should have. Beliefs can sway prosecution decisions! Just warning a mental-health facility, that unknown "actors" would begin arriving, to see if they could fool staff—influenced diagnostic accuracy. Even though no-actors were sent, the staff identified numerous "actors" that they were suspicious of.

POLICE RECOGNITION

FALSE POSITIVE = NON-EXISTENT PATTERN

FALSE NEGATIVE = MISSED REAL PATTERN

If medical experts and their "beliefs" create **abnormals out of normals**, or treat abnormals as normal, then this highlights just how hard law-enforcement has in identifying and dealing with pathological mental-conditions out in the real-world. Mental health officials use **diagnostic labels**, while police use background record checks. Neither of which accurately describes the person right in front of you at this here/now moment, but our belief systems and behavior will be modified by this information. Personal beliefs influence association learning, the way or how you theorize belief-influenced data context meaning supposition "value." "Belief-dependent-realism" flavored by paradigm filters and cultural diversification; as we are pattern recognition social-creatures on a personal mission until we are the last person to die in our lifetime. Police evaluation skills during a routine shift require numerous situations where we cognitively experience a "**false-negative**" (missed a real pattern) and/or a "**false-positive**" (nonexistent-pattern). That is normal investigative police-pattern-recognition. Recognition as a stimulus resulting in fixed-action behavioral patterns.

SELF-AWARENESS OF SELF-CENSORSHIP

For a police-officer on the scene of a complicated emotional incident, seeing reality clearly for what is really there, your wisdom can make or break your success in seeking solutions. If your department or agency is guided by "public-policy" that is counter-productive, un-wise, prejudiced and not welcomed by the community, your response may be doomed from the beginning. R.J. Sternberg describes **"five-fallacies"** concerning your **thought process** that may encourage unintended behavior, especially for law-enforcement: "Unrealistic optimism, egocentrism, illusions of omniscience, omnipotence and invulnerability." All five can get law-enforcement into dangerous situations. Historians warn us that even as wise as Socrates was believed to be, we have no actual written documents attributed to Socrates. Only documents written by his student Plato survived. For some of us, controlling our own emotions may be the wisest choice in their personal development. When you find yourself "**speaking without thinking**," are you finally exposing your true self thought processes, without the self-awareness of self-censorship. Francis Bacon described four obstacles between you and wisdom or "true-knowledge. "Mistaking surface appearance for the true nature of things," "personal preoccupations and obsessions," language as "labels" that are usually not accurate, and "false idols of the theatre." For some, wisdom may merely be recognizing personal desires, to recognize how their desires control over our subconscious thought processes. Investigating wisdom thru philosophical or religious eyes, will result in a different investigation process and findings, than an empirical scientific investigation. For Gerard Brugman, being "**an expert in uncertainty**" is wisdom. Your personal wisdom should be tested through social interaction and social context— "seeing through illusion." What good is wisdom if you never put it to use. Unverified wisdom. How wise do you routinely deal with "contradictions and resolutions." Otherwise, you only have your unverified personal bias about your "wisdom-skills." A "fully-integrated-personality" seems a prerequisite for mastering (development and expressing), "wisdom."

Manifesting never-ending "thought" quantity, does not guarantee quality. Have you seriously examined your (responsibility)

"patterns-of-behavior" and "dysfunctional assumptions" that you have about yourself and all your citizen-interaction? Your personal habits of interpretation, the negative aspects, concerning your citizen-interaction may be easily detected by your co-workers, yet not admitted to, or even recognized by yourself. Make a quick but thorough list of all your habits that infect your citizen-interaction, especially personal habits that you recognize as counterproductive. Looking back at your career in law-enforcement, did you have any trainers, leaders or partners who you felt were truly "wise?" Because you thought these individuals wise, does that make them really wise? Think back to this "wise" person you were so fortunate to have interacted with professionally in law-enforcement. Would any of the following describe this person? Strong reasoning ability, compassionate, balanced, honest, pragmatic, concern for others, impulse control, exceptional cognitive basis for police-work, observant, logical thinking, flexible, knew his or her own limitations, policing knowledge, open-minded, policing experience, problem solving motivation and abilities, insight, intuition, willingness to recognize incorrect decision making and correct it, strong when appropriate—guidance skills, perceptive judgment, sympathetic, reflective attitude, emotional intelligence, friendliness, has learned from mistakes past, peaceful when appropriate for the job, has humor, solved citizen interaction problems instead of avoiding or passing them on to others, self-acceptance, openly recognizes that different-points-of-view are a constant for law-enforcement, uncertainty is dealt with appropriately, social-intelligence, ability to accurately differentiate citizen mental-states that need attention prioritized, conscientious, anticipate reactions of others, recognizes paradoxes, recognizes contradictions and compromise, situational specifics, motivated to find common good, strong predictive powers, shared community interest, offers cooperative citizen strategies in conflict resolution, maturation of self-regulation, recognizing a societal dependency on others, calm while citizens promote "diametrically opposite conclusions," understands the long-range effects of decisions made, does not force his religious views on citizens, understands the potential effects of negative memes, "openness to experience," fluid with critical reflection in a timely manner, transcends individual concerns, a productive style of personal interactions, creative—especially with novel ideas for unusual citizen interactions, rarely self-absorbed in public.

BELIEFS LIMIT CLEAR THINKING

Martial artist Peter Ralston, in his book "Principles of Effective Interaction," describes how early in his career, he determined that he had to "pursue the Truth, instead of any BELIEF SYSTEM." Do not just examine your belief systems to verify they are really worth expending energy, mind and body. Go beyond the BELIEFS you energize, yet never verified the effectiveness and truth behind them. Do not just hope and wish for this analysis, actually intend this necessary and life-changing mind-set. Thoughts with "feeling" become subconscious beliefs, you may not recognize as ever choosing such a belief. Dr. Joseph Murphy reminds us that your "beliefs" and "profoundest convictions," so firmly rooted in your subconscious mind, are almost impossible to consciously describe or defend, as it is neuronally "written" in your subconscious mind as fact/belief—no investigation needed. There is no "arguing" because you don't recognize a "conflict" that needs "change." Many times, we find that the "master" in their field of expertise has "failed more times than the student has tried" (Mac Duke). Do your beliefs limit your thought processes, strategies, ambition and ultimately ensnare and trap you in behavior that you are not proud of and intentionally ignore? The "solution" is so simple, that we rarely even believe it can work, so we do not even try. We must **"change our mind!"** All the self-help books in some way, encourage you to just "change your mind." If you can't even "change your mind," how can you as law-enforcement change the mind of the citizenry we are required to interact with during one of the worst times in their lives.

Sometimes at complicated emotionally violent incidents, law-enforcement retreats to an attitude of as-trained "**strategy**" (checklist of pre-determined guidance "must-do" for personnel and equipment positioning) as more prioritized "important," instead of the actual interaction ultimate "objective" for this particular incident. It is easier to "question" the interpretations of others, than your own. The old military-intelligence quote about needing to know what is actually out there, not what we (beliefs) merely think or hope is out there. Do your police-behavior **habitual patterns of action** stimulus-responses reflect your training preparation, more than the actual "meaning" of the dispatch, reality-on-scene, you are trying to decipher? I am more inclined to believe neuroscientists who claim that talking to yourself is healthy, even though it does not make sense to me. Why do we talk to ourselves about stuff we obviously already know? I am not talking about studying for a test, self-mental exams. Dr. Murphy reminds us that we can intend **positive programming** that can arise to conscious awareness when needed. Is your "subconscious—WILL" stronger than your "conscious—WILL?" When you choose to maintain attention on environmental-stimuli, do you just attend to your attention longer, or intend a mental-force like will? With the power of your subconscious operating out of your awareness, can you be sure your subconscious is not sabotaging your efforts to improve your life, especially citizen-interaction?

FALSE INSTINCTIVE BEHAVIORAL RESPONSE

Anxiety, a rehearsal of fear, and your mental-search for causal affect, influences our behavior, even for the best of us. Asocial thoughts, urges and wishes as mental processes, do not injure or harm your community. It's what you do with those thoughts, urges and wishes. Citizens, and especially police-officers, when under stress and no-longer feeling in control of their lives; are evolutionarily-designed to "**perceptually**" **regain their objective ideation** of seemingly being in control. This means errors in "pattern-detection." We begin seeing imaginary outside-stimuli, "illusory-pattern-perception." Our mood may feel better, but illusory patterns can create false instinctive behavioral responses, including weapon use, all based on imagination, not reality. Feelings of "lacking-control" automatically initiate increased interrelationship associations concerning outside-stimuli, "**patternicity**" that may not really exist. An interesting clinical investigation into illusory pattern perception utilized computers to "evaluate" correct or incorrect answers concerning a real pattern or non-existent pattern. The computer actually just randomly identified (randomized feedback), a subjects answer as correct or incorrect, inconsistent with actual reality. This investigation clearly revealed that the subjects tested thru randomized computer feedback, clearly felt less-in-control, and perceptually detected illusory patterns more often.

Pissed-off police-officers are evolutionarily designed to regain control of their lives, even if this means increased false patterns being imagined; altering their behavior responses and increased potential for error, less potential for error-detection behavioral modification. Law-enforcement is further snared by feelings of no-longer-being-in-control, because it has been proven that **previous unrelated incident responses** will be "pattern-linked" into your thought pattern analysis, contaminating unrelated here/now police investigations. This "**illusory-correlation**" has been proven to infect nonexistent relationships. We automatically overestimate this illusionary relationship in our search for "control," potentially using violent self-affirmation to prove-our-self-righteous-point! Dr. Michael Shermer provides a definition of "agenticity" that relates to law-enforcement: "Agenticity—The tendency to infuse patterns with meaning, intention, and agency." While on patrol we usually effortlessly determine "**inanimate-forces**" from "**intentional agents**" out-of-our-awareness. While sneaking-up on suspects in any environment, I utilized the distraction and noises of inanimate-forces to conceal my approach, an option that criminals can also utilize against us. Army snipers can slow-drag-and-crawl all-day to get to their ideal sniping position. Inanimate forces can "scare" you as powerfully as intentional agents, especially if you entertain thoughts of "supernatural" influence. My first tour of Korea was as an Army MP "Tower-Rat" private E-nothing, guarding nuclear weapon components. We were a prime target for terrorists and the North Koreans. We routinely had evidence of North Korean agents around our camp. For the overnight shift, our tiny movie-theatre moved longer-movies to earlier starting times. Otherwise, no-one on the overnight shift could see the movie—cutting into profits. Sometimes, after a sci-fi thriller got me all shook-up, I would lock-and-load my M-16 after being dropped off at the bottom of the hill where my tower was located. I would be more alert while distractedly falsely-nervous searching for patterns, because of a scary movie, more than any real North Korean provocation. Belief-dependent-realism?

SOCIAL-CREATURE UNEASY INTERACTION

Your subconscious accepts as truth all thoughts you do not correct or challenge. Your subconscious has no operating choice—these new thoughts, raw, unrefined and unverified, are programmed to become your reality, whether ultimately helpful or not. It is nice to think about becoming a better member of law-enforcement in the future, but here/now is where it really occurs. Quoting Dr. Murphy: "Imagination is your most powerful faculty," (especially for actualizing potentialities, the ambiguous and the clearly intended). "Imagine what is lovely and of good report. You are what you, "directed-mental-effort," imagine (causality) yourself to be." Your "mental-triggers" need to be identified before you activate (causal-efficacy), your weapon's trigger—effortless volitions determined out of your awareness, all behaviorally pre-programmed. Know thyself, especially thy-self-censorship skills and thy-veto-powers. Is it possible that your "conscious" self has been silenced and

115

imprisoned by your "subconscious" self? The first step in escaping false imprisonment, is recognizing that you are imprisoned! What behavioral experience is your subconscious compelling you, neuronal architecturally route-determined, empowering pre-programmed behavioral expression? Is "volition" merely attention disguised? You find yourself on a subconsciously empowered ride (urge-to-act) of your own programming—or, perhaps ignorant pre-programming. Your **interaction with the environment is your "behavior."** We have long lost the behavioral intention (readiness-potential) to serve humanity as a priority in our life; it has become secondary, while we maintain well-intended community-oriented perspectives over self-reflective-priorities? We sooth ourselves by believing that we tried, but present circumstances, unconscious-neural-states, and other forces made such a "Mother Theresa" lifestyle impossible for my law-enforcement career. We tried! Considering all the uncontrolled thoughts each of us have, that ramble around ambiguously prioritized, reaching sacred "conscious" recognition; we further "skillfully" or not, express the special-thoughts out-loud—your life's initiatives and priorities, (past-present-future), verbalized through meaningful-symbolic noises, in our social-creature-moments of uneasy interaction.

QUIETING YOUR MIND

Experts remind us that all we need to do to see reality as it really is, is to initiate or intend to begin "cessation of active opposition" on the part of your "objective or conscious mind." That is all, yet it can be one of the hardest processes to maintain, as we automatically regress back to our old ways of thinking and seeing the world, especially citizen-interaction. The less based in reality your non-stop inner-mind chatter takes you, the more easily you will be receptive and vulnerable to the deceptive subjective impressions and falsehoods of others. One of the toughest parts of law-enforcement for me, was how often citizens lied to me. When the thoughts of others enter your thought processes without being verified as true, these thoughts will always lead to **unconscious beliefs**. Beliefs, that you usually do not even realize you hold as auto-truths that direct and influence your citizen-interaction. Your unconscious mental processes have innated and **socially influenced architecture** design that controls how you see the world, determines how you interact with the world, and how you emotionally feel about your citizen-interaction, now and as mental memory residue—context and category. That unhelpful mental memory residue injected into your thought processes by someone else, not only becomes a "belief," but it becomes an "**image in your mind**." This questionable image will be "intuited" as true, to the point that you defend, promote and energize automatically, without reservation—sometimes without intention or control—someone else's thought pattern without knowing or recognizing what you have "really" experienced—or know to be true. "It's alive" in your head! Have you ever tried quieting your mind. Just simply not encourage any thoughts. Just see what pops into your head and do not react or force. Just let thoughts slip away. Without effort, I can only go a minute without thoughts popping in my head. The Buddhists ask **where do thoughts** come from? Most of us have allowed others "thoughts" to be what auto-arises to our conscious awareness, over our own personal thoughts, mental-health, needs, wants, desires.

HABITUAL MOTIVATION OVERRIDES

WHAT YOU REALLY INTEND

I had to swear an oath, before working many of my jobs. Consider the following: "Affirm" your intentions to regain control of your thought processes. Prepare a paragraph specifically for your situation and "affirm" while sincerely maintaining an attitude of true intent. Although you can share this affirmation with others, it is not really necessary if you are truly attempting to regain control of your thought processes. This includes all the time we waste avoiding self-improvement and other positive companion thought processes. Try to grasp the difficulty in determining just <u>how much</u> <u>of your mental-life</u> **"is subconscious,"** especially where this out of your awareness process—takes you! When you respond to your thoughts habitually, (conditioned by your thoughts), thoughts have become an "action." Habitual motivation overrides what you really intend. During citizen-interaction, the citizen is not responsible for the way you think about them. Citizens as well as police-officers, can detect being lied to, maybe even your silent body-language communication display reveals deceit. What <u>citizen-interaction</u> <u>"habits"</u> do you behaviorally act-out are consciously intended. What citizen-interaction "habits" do you behaviorally act-out from your subconscious storehouse of beliefs and interpretation of reality? Intending to harmonize your conscious and subconscious mind, should not be interpreted as a threat by the subconscious. "Fears" without a basis in reality. Many fairy tales play humans as "creatures of habit." Can you recognize any "subconscious-obstacles" in your life? Survival requires subconscious "fear-thoughts" to alter your behavior, out of your awareness. Are you "above" actually forming conscious positive thoughts or suggestions, for programming your subconscious?

<u>SUSPENDING YOUR EGO</u>

Peter Ralston reminds us that "mastery" of any skill "is about **relationship**." Mastering a skill like law-enforcement—citizen interaction, requires actual "other-people." You can't reliably evaluate your "mastering" law-enforcement skills, without actual citizen interaction—in both positive and negative situations. "Change" is inevitable, do not fight it. Master "change." If you cannot "control your mind," don't be alarmed. Almost everyone you meet daily has never even considered taking charge of their own wandering and rambling mind-thought processes. What you "think" you are facing out on the streets, may not be what "really" is out there. In martial-arts, during a fighting-match, **"surrendering-to experience"** is best. Law-enforcement may not like the "surrendering" part, yet it is not negative. It is truly experiencing what is before your eyes to determine what is effective at that moment, not what was effective three weeks or two years ago. Remain in the here-and-now. For law-enforcement, merely "**letting-go**" is the hardest law-enforcement skill most of us have to learn. If you do not learn to "let-go" of a prior incident response, the negative aspects of each incident will pile-up and cloud your mind. Law enforcement is equipped with "**auto-judge**" thought processes that taint reality as it really is. We mean well as we arrive on the scene. A truly professional response requires "suspending your ego" effortlessly and automatically for your next citizen-interaction gambit.

Besides our "auto-judge" tendencies (good aspects/bad aspects), we as law-enforcement cannot truly evaluate our **citizen-interaction-relationship-response**, if we only evaluate the end result—ignoring the journey that led to the end result. Some law-enforcement shifts seem to be remembered only thru "end-result" statistics, especially the bad things that happened to us and at us. How we describe an incident later may stir up internal negative emotional thoughts, but those thoughts are not the real incident. How did you get to the "end-result," of the incident you were dispatched to. You have an unconscious interpretation of "physical-laws" that pre-programs your motor-behavior—for you. Are they based only on speculative guestimated "subjective-experience," instead of physical-objectivity based reality? Your unconscious mental library of physical-law expectations and beliefs, act as additional filter-influencers during your face-the-world citizen-interaction approach and withdrawal behavior—especially moods of obsessive or compulsive career-ending behavioral choices. Your prefrontal cortex will be activated thru truly-intended "**willed-mental-effort**" action-programs. What part of your brain unconsciously activates (triggers) unconscious unintended mental-effort out of your awareness—infecting your police-choose-a-proper-course of action, behavior? For "whose" volitional purpose or benefit?

INTEGRATING EMOTIONAL EXPERIENCE

SELF-FOCUS INTENDED DIRECTED MENTAL FORCE

During your police-citizen interaction, does your habitual unconscious spontaneous reflexive behavior calm or worry the citizen? Are they reflective of environmental-cues, or more reflective of the distracting unrelated conversation you are having with yourself in your head—struggling to affirm, confirm, justify and defend your bias and belief unconscious mental-library. Damage to the prefrontal cortex has been proven to result in the inability to control inappropriate behavioral responses for the sensory stimuli you interact with in real-life, not your minds subjective version. You are designed to recognize sensory stimuli through conscious sensory awareness, and thankfully, most sensory input is processed unconsciously. How reality based is your visual association cortex and your auditory association cortex. Association skills, at least for my aging friends and family, seem to be the first **interactive interpersonal skill** to lose functionality. If your symptoms of mental-distress, included incomplete "integrating emotional experience" with sensory-input; unable to extract "contextual-information" from your sensory-input; while conscious-awareness of all sensory-input is no longer under volitional control—and more confusing than helpful; you probably would not even recognize a problem. It would take a "other" in your life, to alert your "self." Do you feel confident that you would recognize the above perceptual-malfunction symptoms in yourself, citizens and co-workers? What kind of "directions" do you prepare self-focus-instruct "**directed-mental-force**" you initiate, or do you just unconsciously hope for the best? Do you have any real control over the effort (strength/duration) what you focus on, and why you initiate or terminate random focusing?

120

To truly "master" your law-enforcement citizen interaction requires admitting where you could have tried something different, spoke clearer and energize more emotionally secure citizen-interaction. Don't wait for another law-enforcement officer to step-in and question your mind-set at the last citizen-interaction event you experienced. Don't wait for someone else to motivate you. Do you have "unrealistic citizen-interaction fantasies?" Not the sexual kind. Simple everyday citizen-interaction—what citizen problems or issues do you feel justified to ignore and forget? Leaving them for someone else to help, assist and motivate—not real citizen-interaction. Citizens respond to **mental pain** based on their own personal learned behaviors and library of emotional responses. Citizens respond to physical pain based on their own personal learned behaviors. Law-enforcement responds to **physical pain** based on their own personal and professional, learned behaviors. Most of your "learned-behaviors" developed subconsciously without your awareness (programmed by others), especially during childhood. You don't really know what you have stored—waiting for thought processes to expose bits and pieces. Emotionally violent police-investigations usually become counter-productive when you lose control of just which bits and pieces you expose. Only you know your real "perception-of-pain" experience, and a separate "perception-of-pain" as memory process. Citizen-interaction with a psychogenic sufferer (real-pain?), may unfortunately be more dictated by department budgets and time a patrolman can consume, to decipher what is best for society or the citizen? We routinely smile and back away from a citizen because we have calls backed up. They may have told the strangest false story you have ever heard, but we diagnose them as "psychogenic" and walk away. Unless they are hurting themselves and others, we move on wondering how they survive as well as they do.

EMOTIONAL MEMORY FORMATION

Your happiness, self-interest, feeling comfortable and secure, is more positively influenced by cooperation than control. Are you brave enough to confront personal anxious self-absorption in yourself? Do you allow **negative thoughts** to appear and disappear all day, without ever questioning the validity or usefulness of such thoughts? If you cannot stop your never-ending default mode of negative thoughts, experts encourage you to just replace the "anti-you" thoughts with positive thoughts—about yourself and others. Emotional memory formation coupled with a damaged amygdala. The "medical-process" for medication to affect cellular processes is fairly identifiable and routine. It is an entirely different more complicated process for medication to influence behavior. Do you consider simple "happiness" a "reward?" One of the oldest parts of your brain, the limbic-system, if injured or surgically manipulated, shows the importance of this "emotional-brain" concerning thoughts of happiness and reward. Losing your ability to plan or understand "reward" concepts, can end a career in law-enforcement. Every "visual-problem" that a police-officer recognizes at complicated events, will remain visual-problems/information. Understanding and solving these visual problems prove extremely difficult when you are "medically" blocked from connecting the visual problem with an end-game solution. Your citizen-interaction with someone reported to be displaying "behavioral abnormality," may reveal the primary cause not to be medical issues or biological abnormality. This particular citizen just wants to fight someone or blame someone for something, and "tag-your-it." The person who has to solve this situation. Neuroimaging has shown that just prior to someone experiencing **auditory hallucinations**; the parts of the brain necessary for generating inner speech, are activated in such a manner, that the individual is not aware that they self-generated the auditory hallucination out of their awareness. When working properly, your intent to form words and speak, this "efferent copy" is compared by "comparator" mental processes. If this "efferent

122

copy" is not processed normally, the human host will recognize this as proof of abnormal external alien thoughts not generated by the human host—even though it was human-host generated.

SURVIVAL-BASED POLICE ACTION

Beliefs you are absolutely convinced to be true, may still be proven to be delusional misidentification. If you are not aware that you are experiencing repression and dissociation concerning any traumatic memories you hold, you will not associate your unusual or unexplained behavior with these same traumatic memories. The biggest influence on your belief formation and associated preoccupations, may not be the truth behind that belief, but the "**encoded**" emotional state you were in when you formed that particular belief. A belief you may have formed and entered into memory without your conscious awareness or verification. Take the time to understand how your "explicit" memories are subdivided into "declarative" and "episodic" memories. Understand how "implicit" memories are subdivided into "emotional" and "procedural" memories. Procedural memories mandate motor memories and subsequent behavior—habitual reactions, even "**survival-based actions**". Once you clearly understand these differences, the power of your unconscious will increase your opportunities at utilizing these skills more positively and rewarding for yourself and the citizens you interact with. Understanding the different skillsets involved with implicit and explicit memory systems, will decrease the negative influence of traumatic events we respond to. For law-enforcement, episodic memories influence your success in police responses and "**survival advantages**." New police-officers are trained to just "follow department procedures" and you will do fine. New recruits should understand exactly what "procedural memories" mandate in every police response we make. Every time you respond to an incident, you attach meaning to that police-response. Your personal, hidden from others, memories of your actions, and the actions of every other participant, will be significantly influenced by the meaning you attached (interpretation) at that moment, usually as an unconscious process. We also find that the meaning you attached to the incident, can be altered during the "process of recall," what experts call a "ongoing adaptive process." If you get emotional at the crime scene, that mood further sends your mind to every related or associated memories and thoughts you have stored, that have nothing really to do with what you are doing at that moment. How you organize this incoming raw-data in your mind can be negatively influenced, if not blocked by your undisciplined mind. Your current citizen encounters will always be influenced by your historical memories, attitudes and intentions; just make sure that you are always aware (conscious awareness) of how your past influences are determining your present moment behaviors.

CAUSAL DETERMINATION

PROBLEM SOLVING MENTAL MECHANISMS

Tacit knowledge. Experts have analyzed decision-making processes involving your military experience of complex emotional events for analysis and improvement. This "**tacit knowledge**" was not really disseminated to law-enforcement thru command directives, but it was reaching the patrol supervisory level. It was relayed by the large number of formerly military personnel, now working in law-enforcement. Every response is different, requiring a slightly modified approach that worked in the past. With the right training, experience and personality, you can "flow" into de-escalation and excellent citizen interaction and opinion polls. Re-energizing your tacit knowledge related to your military service, into your present-day police work, is not militarizing the police. Decision making when not fully-informed, probably being deceived by someone, and under enormous time-constraints with backed-up calls waiting, is difficult. Selling excess military equipment to local police, if not done right or with good-intentions, is militarizing the police. (I did not agree with

124

Indianapolis Indiana police utilizing military grade vehicles to raid grandmas doing bingo in their basement, or grandpas playing poker in a house garage!) Your department's predictive theories concerning future needs, equipment and manpower, greatly influence theories and assessments concerning what you expect to interpret and experience in this imagined future. Your **interaction with the public** can always be improved, but first you have to admit to yourself you need improvement—like most social animals do. Your police-citizen interaction requires causal-determination, "intuitive reasoning" and "problem-solving mechanisms," while leaving the citizen with a sense or perception of control.

While on patrol, you have mental-narratives deep in your head in your attempt to **determine "meaning"** concerning some event you just witnessed. This meaning "means" that you have to develop goal-oriented behavior based on your decision-making skills. If you do not overcome your biases, you will introduce them into every police-citizen interaction you make. You use **mental-shortcuts (heuristics)** and other cognitive-bias-shortcuts to speed up your citizen interaction meaning-making experience. Logical fallacies based on bad logic and false premises, are not always innocent. Subjective experience emotional evaluation, yourself and others, may be the first decision-making processing you conduct, probably out of your awareness. "Priming" is an important concept that law-enforcement should be aware of. Your perception processes, when analyzed by your unconscious out-of-your awareness; motivate these "priming" adaptive unconscious affects, that **will trap you in past mind-states**, that have nothing to do with the reality of the situation you were dispatched to. Your unconscious, once "primed" by a previous experience, will alter your behavior out-of-your awareness. Every outside-stimuli you perceive triggers **"associations,"** real, or imagined—ambiguity-based hidden-bias behavior. Rational and primal-emotions in mental combat are empowered when you are patrolling on "autopilot." You are influenced out-of-your awareness by your emotional brain. The only signs you detect may be strange intuitions or feelings that may seem out-of-place. We usually cannot consciously self-analyze <u>how our emotional-primal-brain is influencing our rational brain</u>. The untrained distracted Police-officer may be surprised what motivated behavioral lottery of the moment, pops up! In David McRaney's wonderful book, YOU ARE NOT SO SMART, he encapsulates this hard to believe "PRIMING" affect on all-of-us, as **"You are unaware of how unaware you are."**

"Perception sounds like a fancy way of talking about sensing, but it is a useful term because it makes the distinction that we are never in direct contact with the real world. Everything we see, hear, touch, taste, or smell has been filtered and distorted by the pathways leading to our conscious experience of life. Yet, as the description of vision has shown, despite the fragmentary processing, we feel that we see a whole and intact world, or rather, we gloss over the cracks and believe that we are seeing a 20/20 view-of-life." From THE APE THAT SPOKE by John McCrone.

CONDITIONAL PROBABILITY JUDGMENTS

Goals remain only goals, when they are <u>only</u> represented in your mind, and not yet realized. Sometimes we evaluate unconsciously, potential consequences of our goals determined under uncertain conditions, that change as fast as we make decisions. Experts describe that **"visceral states,"** that may only be recognized by you as feelings and emotions, play a critical role in complex behavior you interpret as necessary to deal with the meaning and labels you determined. Your departments influence on you is determined by three attributes; values stressed, a never-ending list of assumptions about your community and expected police-behavior, especially what past historical aspects of your department that are promoted or censored. What part of your work-performance is more "role-filling" rather than "role-playing." If you cared more about the public, would that increase your personal emotional issues? Every decision we make, unconsciously or consciously, adds conditions (**conditional probability**) to how we interpret future interaction, especially instantaneous attentional-judgments. We have created mental images of probability-judgments out of our own awareness.

"Then man's ancestors happened on the trick of language. Suddenly, a whole new mental landscape opened up. Man became self-aware and self-possessed. He broke free of the grip of the present—the moment-to-moment life lived by all other animals—and became master of his own memory. Language allowed man to relive his past, plan for the future, and step back to consider the fact of his own existence. Through speaking, man rapidly developed a self-conscious mind." From THE APE THAT SPOKE by John McCrone.

Scientists have even created a "geometric" approach using complex model thought-processes involving "**personal-preferences**." After reading their material multiple times, it is obvious I am unable to determine the viability of almost anything geometric or quantum described. Law-enforcement observing "categorical variables" and "random variables," always aware of socio-cultural "**interference-effects**." Law-enforcement even has our own version of the physics "law of reciprocity." An officer interprets that something observed requires a police response (interference), and the citizenry will "**transition-probability**" in expected escape "opposite-directions." You can plan ahead to limit the "terms-of-transition" options available for the citizen you are targeting for direct interference. Decisions for altering your response will be based on unconscious decisions and expectations already encoded as memory, and part of your "belief" system of unchecked and unverified belief systems. Similar to a quantum scientist, an officer mentally "interprets" stimuli utilizing "complete" measurements and "coarse" measurements. Quantum scientists also utilize investigative tools similar to observing "incompatible events" involving citizen "non-commuting projectors."

"The essential threat violence poses are that the actors in the violent situations go past one another, do not learn from one another how to change their questions, their objectives, their senses of the problems, of what is important to know. People protect their privacy with acquaintances, let alone strangers, by telling others what they think is safe and acceptable for them to hear. A façade of peace may easily conceal violent interaction, while loud complaints may cover a situation where conflict is encouraged and democratically managed." From The Geometry of Violence and Democracy, by Harold E. Pepinsky.

Advances in electromagnetic induction lead into **transcranial magnetic stimulation** (TMS) investigations into psycho-neural substrates and neuroanatomical hypothesis. Muscular activity can be activated by TMS when positioned over the primary motor cortex. Brief flashes of light will be neuronally imaged (not to be confused with "imagining), in the absence of external visual stimulus. Neuroscience has developed the capability to **manipulate human specific frequency** (by task) utilizing "selective-disruption." They disrupt your normal routine cortical networks frequency down to the "task" level.

CHAPTER FOUR

AUTOMATIC HABITUAL EMOTIONAL ROULETT

POLICE REACTIONS

For some police-officers, their ultimate addiction is "control." I am talking about "control" beyond routine—necessary aspects of law-enforcement citizen-interaction, control for societies sake—not personal grudges. Yes, we are empowered by the government to "control" situations, when we have to; but, do not become a fear-based "control-freak" (self-imposed rituals-compulsions and obsessions) during the most routine of citizen-interaction. Experts report that your brain abhors ambiguity, and automaticity takes place, desperately filling in the gaps in order to determine "meaning" and "patterns." Law-enforcement behaviors based on automatic habitual emotional roulette reactions—are usually out of your conscious control, making you more vulnerable to suggestions from others. As your motivated-behavior occurs, illogical to outsiders, you will automatically support the illogical-behavior by providing "**fictional-narratives**" that you believe properly explain your behavior—to yourself and others. This is comparable to "split-brain confabulation." Is your "sense-of-self" as a "confabulatory-creature," getting you into situations you don't like, over-and-over? Your stream-of-consciousness as a "flow," is a separate mental-process from recognition or thinking about what images dance around in your mind. Your "values" are not universally prioritized, and get even more complicated when you unconsciously add your "labels" and your interpretation of "values" to your descriptions of events and behavior involving others. Your **values motivate behavior** just as effectively as your negative side—especially when involved in "**conflict-resolution.**"

Internationally, conflict-resolution became a major topic at the end of the cold-war. My two tours with 8th Army in Korea, and two tours with 7th Army in Europe were documented in my previous book,

POLICE COLD WAR. From the outside (to me), it appeared that more modern international conflicts were tempered by conflict-resolution techniques. A welcome and genuine attempt to empower the powerless in the face of growing threats and over-whelming economic and military might, from bigger more powerful countries seeking regional or global domination. These larger more dominate players **control the press** and more <u>easily determine the information narrative disseminated back to the world</u>—especially what is considered a failure or success. Please take the time to watch the documentary "<u>THE GHOSTS OF ABU GHRAIB</u>." The tragedy of ABU GHRAIB was not only a stain on the U.S. Army, it really destroyed the image of Military Police! The reservist were only MPs, who were not trained in correction-duties. They were put in charge of the worst prison at the time, in the entire world—in a combat-zone. The Army conducted over 100 investigations not designed to find the truth and fix procedural errors and outright criminal-conduct. The investigations were only designed to find ways to keep upper-level management from having their careers ruined because of their promotion of the very same techniques used. I was warned back in the late 1970s by MI staff that <u>MPs were used in Vietnam as scapegoats</u>—should enhanced techniques become public.

"When we or others in our interaction pursue an objective compulsively, we feel a threat to our survival. We feel tension, we feel stress and we feel impending death. The violent tension makes people conservative; ritual becomes hardened. People try harder to stay in place and to put others in theirs. People's objectives become rigid; discipline becomes the order of the day. This is to say the opposite of synergy happens—entropy, or heat. Violence is social entropy, social heat. War and crime cannot be legislated or enforced away. This makes the contribution of any human being to violence or peace supremely important, and evolution from a culture of violence to one of peace fitful and painfully slow. From THE

GEOMETRY OF VIOLENCE AND DEMOCRACY by Professor Harold E. Pepinsky

INCOMPATIBLE GOALS

CONTENT OR RELATIONSHIP CENTERED?

Conflict resolution includes conflict prevention internationally and locally—hopefully before law-enforcement has to get involved. As well intended that international conflict-resolution was initiated around the world, there have been criticisms of the actual results. Some of the "powerless," have identified **"conflicts" in "conflict-resolution"** at the international level. It appears that conflict-resolution involving international relations recognized (disguised) as "stabilizing- successes," may have merely further entrenched "powerful" global forces and the elite as masters in their world-domain where we inhabit. At the local level, where law-enforcement is required to implement conflict-resolution during complex-interplay dispatches involving systemic-complex violent incidents; are our "conflict-resolution-successes;" **community-positive**, or just **law-enforcement positive**? Are identified "incompatible-goals" always favoring the powerful? Just when you successfully got both sides of an issue in agreement, a third-party out of no-where reminds you that community conflict-resolution involves more than only two-sides. Which has worked best for you and your community out on-the-streets; successful conflict resolution, or successful conflict transformation? If you understand the difference for your specific situational successes—pass-it-on! Was your process more **"content-centered" or "relationship-centered."** Do all disputes have to be settled? How often do we merely de-escalate a conflict, and not pursue constructive change through our leadership skills? The antecedent for the "conflict" you were dispatched to figure out, may have evolved over 1000 generations, and probably impossible to solve the "big-picture;" so, you address and prioritize your de-escalation skills for the smaller skirmish right-in-front of you. Avoid only paying attention to information that supports your primed initial "beliefs," while information that contradicts your initial beliefs, conscious and unconscious beliefs; is filtered and bathed in "confirmation bias." "FACTS" that police develop are socially-expressed, socially-defined and interpreted, socially-distorted and manipulated, potentially merely confirmation-bias in-action. Most of us only watch news channels that endorse our ambiguous views and beliefs.

For a responding police-officer, to initiate an investigative-plan and response, we need to determine if the "conflict" we are approaching is a **"destructive" or "constructive"** community-conflict. Sometimes, upon arrival, immediately empowering the participants in the "conflict" in some novel-way, may be more beneficial than immediately relying on brute overpowering force. Now you are intending and dealing with a **"constructive" community conflict**, which usually influences non-violent processes, and a calmer—less weapon-discharge, getting more positive, environment. In a college class, we were encouraged to see conflict as considered from a "consensual" point-of-view; when police-officers respond to an incident involving citizens wanting to purchase declared "illegal" drugs, other products and "special" illegal "services" not legalized that a capitalist consumer would actually prefer. Some conflicts can be seen from a "dis-sensual" aspect when citizens seeking to illegally obtain items of value from other citizens without their permission, in their search to meet their ambiguous and changing daily needs. Life is a "constant mutual interplay between theory and practice" as Oliver Ramsbotham described. It was common for me, to be thinking secretly in my head, "you stupid-idiots are fighting over this?" Minor incidents which sometimes are easily solved by any 3rd party and some common-sense, not just law-enforcement. If you make just a little more effort, you find that you can **solve disputes and problems in advance** related to this subject of investigation and the people involved. The next time you respond to the same area the citizens you positively interacted in the previous incident with, are more friendly—even smiling. I detected that "embarrassment" was being internally felt inside their minds, probably for the first time since childhood. I'll keep this positive and not mention that there are some community members who will never comply with any presented option. *If observation affects the outcome, we aren't merely part of the universe, but participants in it. From the book WHAT THE BLEEP DO WE KNOW.*

NEGATIVE PANIC—FEAR-BASED IMMOBILITY

Sometimes it just feels good to allow consoling "hindsight bias" when you internally recognize that your cause-and-effect "predictions" didn't quite work out; but, is this "stress-release" ethical? Experts stress that "meaning is a human construction." You will have to live with the real "reality" of your predictions that did not work out, no matter how much you cultivate hindsight bias. Humans are experts at detecting patterns, real or imagined—while ignoring that we have inconsistent preferences; remember, we have the ability to **think-about-thinking**, metacognition and improving de-escalation skills. Do you consider yourself a rational being of pure logic? Police-officers are expected to present the emotional-state of super-human calmness in the worst of situations, one of the few positive aspects of *"normalcy-bias."* When a plane is on fire, and a few passengers experience *"negative-panic,"* and remain buckled in their seats, you should snap them out of their procedural stupor, as rigorously as you non-injuriously can, on your way out of the plane. Law-enforcement should easily recognize *negative-panic, fear bradycardia, reflexive incredulity, severity underestimation, introspection-illusion* and *tonic immobility;* before citizen anxiety or fear-based immobility, increases the chances for you and others to get injured.

"The Process-of-Individuation describes the process by which the conscious and the unconscious within an individual learn to know, respect and accommodate one another. The process of individuation is complete, when the conscious and the unconscious have learned to live at peace and to complement one another." From MAN AND HIS SYMBOLS, Carl G. Jung

Law-enforcement responds to many emergency incidents involving in-the-street economic-crimes (robberies/larceny). The overall policies creating (and maintaining) **"economic-differentiation"** in community environments of despair and dual standards, is out of our hands. All law-enforcement has to do is: "We must be resolute in our analysis involving community-conflict at all levels. This includes you, especially you. Your **intra-personal** conflicts—that interpret, motivate and determine for you. The format and architecture behind your neuronally-based behavioral interpersonal interaction involving interpersonal-conflicts; especially what your group-speak considers conflict-resolution "success." What you personally (emotional programming) truly consider success—which influences and is influenced in multiple group-speak/**intergroup** feed-back loops of other police-officers, family and outside group interests—which are heavily influenced by multi-cultural flavored international relations stratagem—all involving "conflict-resolution." That is all! When you initiate law-enforcement designed and implemented conflict resolutions, are these just temporary band-aids that put off true, intended for the community—conflict resolution—that never seem to materialize?

"I have repeatedly seen fights between police and citizens escalate out of an ethos of we versus them, where the primary mission of the police is seen by the police and citizens alike, to subdue and dominate offenders. Law-enforcement escalates disputes within the community. Jailed offenders return home with renewed bitterness and stigma. They and their friends and relatives become adversaries and complainants of police. All in all, dispute management works

best when police substitute mediation and conciliation for enforcement, and police can manage this result only if they become familiar with community residents in context other than law-enforcement." From THE GEOMETRY OF VIOLENCE AND DEMOCRACY, Harold E. Pepinsky.

CONFLICT RESOLUTION—FALSE-SUCCESSES

Experts remind us the potential that this "conflict," originated when the "transformational" "emancipatory discourse" aspect of empowering the powerless, becomes secondary to "settlement" processes that seem to always end up keeping existing power structures in power. You find out that after years of negotiations, the powerful kept their power. The early "successes" deceptively reported in the press, seemed to have become secondary to the actual results. The negative final implemented aspects of "conflict-resolution" can be "bought" in a media that requires advertisement revenue from the same international companies involved in the conflict, and relegated to the back pages if printed or disclosed at all. There is big money to be made in conflict-resolution for the companies that get politically-determined contracts that implement and continue to run these conflict-resolution stratagem budgets around the world. In my mind, as an Army vet with four overseas tours; the two biggest "**war-profiteers**" ever in the United States, was Dick Cheney and the Iraq War Halliburgler scandal, and the private security army known as BLACKWATER. These companies made so much money from the tax-payer, that they were able to legally bribe politicians through campaign contributions and employing their family members and friends. All legal! Who "profits" at the local level from conflict-resolution successes implemented by law-enforcement at all hours of the night. When we choose "**prohibition**" over sane drug-policy, we get the violence and gang-domination such a policy inherently creates, infecting the best of the neighborhoods. I cannot imagine what the drug imported from China, Fentanyl, that kills so many; if it was around in the early 1970s when I was in High School in a very violent period for Gary Indiana. We also know as fact, that China illegally exports Fentanyl similar to their military probes of neighbors and border crossings; as just another way to weaken democracies around the world—who do not live in a police-state like them.

Ineffective citizen-interaction may be based on your false and inappropriate analysis for the situation, labels and values that you assigned. Something in your community has "changed," interpreted as "conflict" immediately, or just simmers out-of-sight, influencing even the most routine of citizen-interaction. Informants are not the best judges of your community—do not become so "occupation" driven, that the only information you receive of value about your community—as a neuronal mental-image, are dual-purpose intent-conflicted driven informants. While a CID Special Agent in Frankfurt, I was Team Chief of the CID Drug Suppression Team, which my medal claimed was the largest-most productive military Drug Team in Europe. Many times, I had to make the difficult choice in not acting on some of our most productive informant's information, because it was always rushed, dangerous, immediate now-or-never disasters in the making. They did not allow proper planning and control—especially involving host-nation law-enforcement. It would have been anti-social for me to create situations almost guaranteeing the need for weapons-pointing when I had the skill and personality to keep most drug-deals friendly with potential repeat customers. Most citizens do not recognize or have to modify their counter-productive behavior for "control" purposes involving others. They either do not care or do not recognize their anti-social behavior as needing modification. Most parents seem to have given up on maintaining control over their own children, and simply hope for the best to magically happen. They leave parental leadership skills to their children's--just as uninformed friends. Some citizens we routinely interact with, seem to exhibit what Dr. William Glaser called **"craziness became an organized behavior;"** their routine mode-of-interaction with the world around them. Citizens approach us with mental constructs in their head concerning what they (control-issues) "want," that contradicts with their interpretation of the situation you responded to. You may be dealing with a citizen who decided that his prescription medication, though seemingly working on his behavior issues, has chosen to stop taking the meds because the side-effects make the slight improved behavioral issues, not worth it. Your brain also generates chemicals for healing and survival.

INCOMPATIBLE OBJECTIVES/UNINTENDED EFFECTS

Police and the citizens we interact with are primed behaviorly to process aversive events, **"unlearned fear" and "learned fear"** as we interact with our environment. All of your "learned-fears," require previously stored **"emotional memory traces"** courtesy of your amygdala and primitive neural circuits in your forebrain. Are you experiencing a "primitive emotional reaction" or a "sophisticated cognitive reaction?" When "attitude" and "behavior" meet "contradiction;" police-citizen interaction becomes interesting— contradiction involving "incompatibility of goals." Being "embarrassed" in public is a big-fear triggering anxiety for some police-officers, which interferes with normal cognitive de-escalation processes—and usually makes you look even sillier. Your "social-values" and "social-structure" are present in every citizen-interaction you make flavored by their "social-values" and "social-structures." Are they set-in-stone and not modifiable nor malleable for this particular situation? During emotional violent incidents, **misperceptions arise without recognition,** more often than you think—elements of undisciplined human behavior, desire, incompatible objectives, bias, beliefs, racial-stereotypes, feelings, human-nature and "conflicts-of-interest" as contributing factors and unintended effects.

Most police-officers have experienced difficulty at complicated incidents involving crowds; where the **core-conflict**, or original reason you responded has been clouded-over, and is now influenced by unnoticed conflicting simmering gestation and a dozen **secondary conflicts**, that you had no way to prepare for and transform. Full-spectrum analysis is alarming your Spidey-senses. How professionally do you modify your behavior when faced with intractable conflict? How are your skills involving peacemaking "evolution of cooperation?" Your" crowd-control" analysis and methodology need to recognize how to change crowd "polarization" into de-escalation successes involving transformation, containment, reconciliation and settlement. Mental health researcher J. Galtung, investigating "**conflict-as-a-way-of-life**" mediation, identified distinctive context and categorical strategies that, for your own sanity, need to be recognized when police-officers respond to **social-dysfunction** in their communities—especially police initiated preventative measures for the future involving accommodation and compromise. We need to recognize before it destroys us emotionally, that some incidents are not best-suited for police-responses as solution-makers—is "yielding" self-interest an option? Do both sides have to win or lose? Mutual retaliation is not uncommon. "Power" plays of interaction reveal emotional baggage that you did not see coming. Police predominately see the "effects" of conflict, rarely the infection that spread it.

SOCIAL EXPLOITATION/CULTURAL INDOCTRINATION

The incident that you just responded to, is it: "Direct-violence?" "Structural poverty type violence?" "Culturally obligated or encouraged violence?" Police are trained and equipped for responding and terminating direct-violence among the citizenry. Reducing tension is an art, especially when intended compensation, concessions and penalties are interpreted. Do we "coerce," "command," and force, or, do we empower, persuade and stepaside? **Social-exploitation** is investigated by culturally indoctrinated social-selves heavily influenced by unconscious mental programming. What looks "weird" or different to one person, may look culturally-normal to another. Cultural and structural issue analysis and arbitration, especially asymmetric conflicts that require more time than we have available during a normal shift—especially preventative awareness education, or even trickier, "conflict-management-issues." Social-change guarantees social-conflict—especially involving emancipatory struggles. I found that if I went out of my way, on my own time, to notify agencies or citizens who could help; just "passing-the-buck" prevented unnecessary worry and concern on my part. We see enough horrible stuff during our shifts. We can proactively remove the negative influence of police-experience as a form of directed self-neural-plasticity skills. Clear minds—save lives—take the first step when no one else will! Your **novel resolution responses** that work—pass them on!

CULTURAL CONFLICTS

Positive citizen-interaction is easy—when you are feeling "positive." Positive proactive citizen-interaction is rarely successful when you are feeling "negative," or even worse; feeling "justified" in feeling worse and self-perpetuating the feeling in self-pity. Promoting "anticipated" "future-mutual-gains" (assimilation advantages) in culturally-diverse conflict resolution, can be legitimately well-intended and meticulously well-presented, and fail because of just one misinterpretation—bargaining bathed in concealment—real or imagined. Suspicion grows propelled by misinformation and culturally mediated propaganda. Cross-culturally mutually accepted? Citizen self-awareness and self-knowledge can help or contaminate—if the source is Q-Anon or a president who refuses to admit he lost an election. **Social identity** is just on-going interpretational mental (self and other) analysis; here/now when we are face to face, countered by outside referenced sources, deceptive, dehumanizing and intentionally scripted cultural context and categorial references taking you out of here/now pure unmediated awareness and attention. Seeing **reality as it really is**, may require changing world views, beliefs and self-questioning ideological orientations as unquestionable ultimate truths—for the better, I hope. Not how one party involved in the conflict wants you to see it. Not how the "powers" want it to be interpreted, documented and reported. Conflict resolution must refine ambiguous **"anticipated" future-issues** influenced by the original conflict-resolution, and understand what their resolution creates in the future—all consequences.

Well-intended "multidisciplinary" participatory approaches can turn into secondary conflicts just involving members of that same "multidisciplinary" group. For one year, myself, Hal Pepinsky, an Indiana University criminology professor who specialized in "Peacemaking," and another similar criminal justice scholar, drove up to Indianapolis for weekly citizen-community discussions concerning local-violence. The group consisted mostly of women-of-color, who were successful in getting senior gang-members to show up. While we successfully interacted with the group members, the gang-members hatred of us (racial/police/justice system), ended up becoming extremely threateningly negative and verbally abusive, that for the group's sake, we stopped attending. After about 15 years of attending a yearly "Sun-Dance" just south of Bloomington, Indiana, I decided to stop showing up for the "group's sake." There were just enough confrontations with attendees upset that I was "white" and participating in the Sun Dance. One upset attendee, a famous indigenous actor, actually grabbed my arm forcefully, to verify that I had the correct "herbs" to counteract the metal in my glasses, for a particular dance. **Global conflicts** do not influence local-community police work; unless you count the protests in your area-of-operation, or influx of unruly crowds, mandatory overtime, businesses forced to close, local-citizens being pushed off the streets and stuff like that.

140

"A paradigm is like the unconscious belief system of a culture. We live and breathe these beliefs, and we think and interact according to them. A paradigm is like a theory, but a little different. A theory is an idea that sets out to explain how something works, like Darwin's theory of evolution. It is meant to be tested, proved or disproved, supported or challenged by experiment and reflection. A paradigm, on the other hand, is a set of implicit assumptions that are not meant to be tested; in fact, they are essentially unconscious. They are part of our modus operandi as individuals, as scientist, or as a society." From the book WHAT THE BLEEP DO WE KNOW

"A paradigm is a grand story or dogma that scientists hold at a given time. Paradigms in science are like dogmas in religion. Champions will protect their respective paradigms virtually at all costs." From THE LIVING ENERGY UNIVERSE, by Gary E. R. Schwartz and Linda G.S. Russek.

SEARCH FOR MEANING—REAL OR IMAGINED

Does **"conflict" require actual physical "behavior?"** Think about how hard it is to understand, really understand social-systems a typical police-officer faces every shift—especially when self-challenging your self-assumptions and bias. We just get a slight taste of various social-systems, never really enough to truly understand that particular social-system (unless it is "ours.") It is the "members" of the social-system in consideration—that continuously learn about their social-system—from each uninformed social-self other. Some less-participatory members may have no more information of value to de-escalate and empower conflict resolution, than the confused uninformed first officer to arrive. It can be hard to disengage with a citizen that you just spent five minutes communicating with, when you realize they know less than you do about the incident. "Simply Solving from Scratch," and on the run—sometimes in dangerous situations. **"Availability-heuristic"** describes police-officers natural reaction tendency problem-solving skills—we auto-contemplate and gravitate to information we are already comfortable with and accustomed to (cultural order or personal synaptic order). This sounds harmless and insignificant, but, cognitive scientists warn us that your unconscious inclination towards comfortable information will be processed faster and more "believable," even if the information was negative-biased, counter-productive and wrong. You will not recognize how you either auto-discarded other information, or do not even recognize the availability or need for more information. Human thinking naturally seeks out "examples" in our search for meaning; real or imagined, in our need to avoid ambiguity in our investigation. If you allow sense-of-self "fear-of-embarrassment" to enter your self-awareness, you will speed up mental-processing and greedily accepting information that comforts your unconscious. You may be experiencing the *"illusion-of transparency"* while nobody is really recognizing your inner-turmoil. To determine outside-stimuli reality-based "meaning," we have to really be receptive and attentive when outside "meaning" is explained by "outsiders." Ultimately, this "meaning," must come from "within," our sense-of-self. After making an arrest with 100% confidence in your decision, police-officers should never experience *post-decisional dissonance*.

Emotional fear may develop from your cognitive analysis of the situation you find yourself in. What Neurobiologist Donald W. Pfaff describes as the "information-processing power of your cerebral cortex." Your frontal cortex is credited with "suppressing sheer fright." We usually think of fear responses as being immediate and efficient. Dr. Pfaff describes that "slow-effect" gene expression ("large proteins that bind stress hormones"), is also utilized to reduce fear responses/feelings. For your **"mechanism of fear"** to continue requires neurochemical and genetic processes. Your **"memory-of-fear"** requires complex "fear-signaling" that begins with the neurotransmitter glutamate. Calcium, phosphorous and oxygen (biochemical cascades/adaptations) and hormonal connections are also required for your memory of fear. The neurobiology of fear also helps you avoid fearful and dangerous situations. Some experts identify that "shared-fear" with the person you are interacting with, is processed subconsciously, and creates mutual thought processes (self/other blurring) to not injure the person you are interacting with—traces of empathy. There is a **"molecular basis" for social recognition"**. Neuropeptides oxytocin and vasopressin harmonize your social interactions into more "friendly-positive behaviors," what Dr. Pfaff called positive "affiliative" behaviors and "a sense of shared fate with another." Obsessive compulsive disorder is now considered a biological disorder, not a psychological disorder. You may occasionally see order in chaos, but do not believe you were "destined" to see it. The more confused you may be, might make you more susceptible to "strange-explanations." Just because you cannot prove otherwise, does not make something possible or responsible—you need to investigate propositions first.

"It can easily be demonstrated that people tend to perceive what they expect to perceive, rather than what is before them. The frailty of human perception is notorious, and it is particularly subject to aberration <u>when the subject and object have some relationship</u>, real or imagined. A perfectly objective analysis of human behavior could not be made by any human being." From HUMAN EVOLUTION, by Bernard G. Campbell

BEHAVIOR IS A FUNCTION OF THE BRAIN

Some police-officers have more difficulty controlling their own behavioral issues during routine citizen-interaction. An angry police-citizen interaction includes ignoring or reframing the citizen's position in neglect—editing the world in our image. While actively listening to "what" the citizen is saying, we need to be aware of "why" they are saying what they say. Guilt-by-association is easily empowered, but, very difficult if not impossible to fully remove false associations from our unconscious memory library. Most incidents that get police-officers in legal trouble occur while trying to "professionally" control others who do not want to actually be "controlled" at that moment. Neuroendocrinologist Dr. Bruce McEwen reminds us that **"Behavior is a function of the brain."** "Walking-away" is a legitimate behavior for law-enforcement when appropriate. One weakness in your training in stimulus-response psychology, is that what you consider responsible reward and punishment criteria for the citizen you are interacting with, is based on your own mental constructs and processes. You may have misinterpreted this citizens behavior or unconsciously confused the citizen with "characters" from social-media and entertainment industry. Our personal version of how we would like to see the world is considered the "JUST (ENTER YOUR NAME HERE) FALLACY."

"Each new content that comes up from the unconscious is altered in its basic nature by being partly integrated into the conscious mind of the observer. Thus, the unconscious can only be approximately described (like the particles of microphysics) by paradoxical concepts." From MAN, AND HIS SYMBOLS by Carl G. Jung

Are you willing to sacrifice a little "power," to reach successful citizen-interaction conclusions. Does the citizen walk away feeling more empowered or pushed aside. Well-intended criticism can be misinterpreted, or worse, be used as the launching pad for your criticism of the other person. Routinely, citizens try to ensnare us in "false-conflicts" of their own creation. **"Control-theory"** advises that when dealing with a true conflict, delaying decisions can help. Most law-enforcement responses do not allow this "delaying-decision" process. Routinely, criticism from another police-officer may sting-more, but criticism from citizens can "set-us-off" more frequently and severely. Even self-criticism can occasionally become overly-critical. When we try to "control our lives" during times of distress and anger, behavioral modification teams up with mental discipline. Author Dr. Glaser describes that behavior is made up of

144

three components: "what we do, what we think, what we feel." Your behavior is your personality. Is your organized "**behavioral system**" at the mercy of outside events? When you recognize that your behavior needs modification, but are emotionally unable to regain control, Dr. Glaser recommends you see your behavior not as one process, but as four components of behavior (doing, thinking, feeling and physiology). Otherwise, <u>you are technically choosing to maintain</u> the "**misery**" of your unhelpful and counterproductive behavior. For some reason we occasionally choose to emit "misery" on those around us. What excuses do you tell yourself when you intentionally choose to ignore an option that would be more effective? Being frustrated is not justification for improper police citizen-interaction (self-destructive and societal-destructive thought processes). You are your own "control-system." Is your "control-system" stimulus-response primarily controlled by "satisfied-yes" or "satisfied-not" wandering undisciplined and untrained thought processes? Do outside forces control your "control-system?" If your "creativity" in citizen-interaction success is "biased," that bias will negatively infect an aspect of your citizen-interaction creativity thought de-escalation processes.

NEGATING POSITIVE CITIZEN INTERACTION

Your behavioral motivation is primarily an internal process. If your behavior is primarily dictated and energized by your reactions and responses first, before your level-headiness has recognized your behavior is making matters worse, something is wrong. On-going behavioral motivation for positive effective citizen-interaction should be your baseline of operation, at all times. Beginning your citizen-interaction from a positive well-intended position, makes recognizing when you are beginning to behaviorally negate citizen-interaction, easier to identify and remedy. If you arrive at an incident already upset, pissed, rushed, near the end of your shift, and distracted, you will not magically calm down without conscious effort. Most of our <u>citizen-behavior evaluation</u> <u>occurs on an</u>

<u>unconscious level</u>, especially concerning "threats," detecting, coping and responding. Which is causing you more difficulty; your pre-programmed presuppositions that arise automatically from your unconscious, or your conscious judgments and interpretations? We have to not only learn to "let-go," of things, but **let-go as a final decision**, and avoid revisiting your personal history of "choices" over and over. That is indicative that your decision was not final. When challenging your own personal emotional behavior, it is recommended that you do not express your behaviors as "nouns." The behavior expressed as a noun, does not describe your behavior. **Expressing your behavior as a "verb"** will help you recognize the "doing and thinking" behind you8r behavior, more than the noun "feeling." Dr. Glaser recommends "angering" instead of anger. He also identifies "smiling," as a "powerful controlling behavior."

SURVIVAL RESPONSES

AROUSAL STATES AND DISTRESS CYCLES

Emotional regulation usually occurs naturally and effortlessly, while some incidents require effort to suppress, reappraise, modulate and modify our emotional reactions in public. Sometimes at complicated emotional incidents, we "deal" with the incident more from an immediate as-it-happens frame-of-mind, where your stored unconscious presuppositions and behaviors occur faster than you can consciously alter them. This is why all your presuppositions need to be reality-based. Dr. Glaser reminds us that the genetic instructions we were born with, require both physical and psychological processes. Law-enforcement (**emotional learning**) needs to be vigilant and recognize when the "**conjunction-fallacy**" has ensnared your unconscious belief systems, and your "expected" interaction-citizen-exchange guarantees what you expect to (inference) happen, more than the real unmediated situation as it really occurs (excitatory/inhibitory balance.) Recognizing psychosocial adversity, social-deficits, negative interference, inferences and errors in your professional "**probability judgments**" can be tamed "amplitude" wise, while your self-healing self-evaluation proceeds (social neuroscience). When your survival responses are based on intense sensations and emotions that you can't seem to gain control over, just recognizing that you have lost control of your own feelings, is the first step in regulating your arousal states. Was this a rare "distress-cycle," or is it becoming a regular occurrence for you. This may work for you, or you may find yourself in a state of profound depression that you cannot identify the source of your trauma. Just make sure that whatever healing method choices you take, you do not develop (consolidation phase) **false memories**, traumatic or regular.

AUTO-CAUSE INTERPRETATION

FALASE-HABITUAL INTERPRETATION

The efficiency of brain metabolism, body chemistry, brain chemistry and especially neurotransmitters that usually function so well, means we never have to think or worry about their viability during our citizen interaction. **Changes in body chemistry are "felt;"** interpreted usually at a subconscious level, which initiates an automatic "response" or "behavior." Your reaction during citizen-interaction and environmental stimuli, can overpower the best of us. Your personal pre-programmed beliefs and expectations will dictate automatic "**pure-feeling-states,**" for which you will have the ability to "choose" what to do, think and further "feel" about the situation. Choosing what to do, think and modify our feelings is a response that we do have control over. While it is usually our thought-interpretation-judgment that pushes us over the edge (brain-states), biochemical imbalances, childhood trauma and future worries may be the basis for behavior you are not proud of. Experts stress that the "experiencer," will not mentally recognize or investigate potential chemical imbalances as a cause of "unhelpful" behavior. We will automatically mentally investigate, detecting "biochemical-in-nature" disturbances; subconsciously and consciously, any patterns indicating "cause or causes" which will be behaviorally prioritized. Just another distraction your own thoughts create. This "cause" will be an interpretation or judgment, right or wrong, helpful or counter-productive. You can become addicted to your cause-interpretation, and automatically overrule reality when your automatic interpretation (habit) proves to be a false habitual interpretation. If you believe your false "cause-interpretation," you will subconsciously believe all outside-stimuli and citizen-interaction you experience, supports and verifies your false conclusions. You will subconsciously block all outside-stimuli and citizen-interaction that runs counter to your false beliefs. Your false beliefs have the power to create the same auto-biochemical events that led to the original false beliefs. A false-belief continuous false-belief loop, out on-the-streets, where it can get you killed or arrested yourself. **Interpretation becomes expectation** in all similar police responses at the unconscious level.

Simple anxiety is considered a normal police response to situations we respond to. A biochemical imbalance can turn simple anxiety into "endogenous anxiety," which is easily treated by big-pharma. Going caffeine free worked for me. Today, in 2023, a major restaurant chain is being sued for two deaths involving their super-charged caffeinated lemonade. The customers did not understand what the "tradename" of the drink really meant. They drank the super-charged caffeinated simple lemonade beverage, and it killed them. I also have a caffeine response that alarms me, body and mind biochemical dimensions. While neurons and synapses get most of the glory, dendrites and their sensitivity to various sets of chemicals is just as amazing. I explored neuron related information in more detail, in my 2nd book, Policing Private Personalities—Preprogramming Positive Proactive Police Phenomenon. As one of my favorite neuroscientists, Michael S. Gazzaniga, put it in his book MIND MATTERS, "The CHEMICAL events that take place at the synapse determine whether or not neural communication continues." Garbage in-garbage out. What do you eat and drink on a regular basis? Think of how much you consume, and how much of it is converted into a chemical-soup for your later use—all without conscious control. How much do you habitually eat and drink based on subconscious impulses (subconscious addictions)? Why? Most scientists investigating message transmissions involving neurons, especially the "biochemical conditions," are psychopharmacologists. Sometimes, excess neurotransmitter release is the problem. Chemical manipulation at the neurotransmitter level. We routinely interact with citizens who are being pharmacologically chemically manipulated. Two methods of chemical manipulation involve manufactured chemicals known as either **agonists and antagonists,** which weirdly mimic personalities of citizens we interact with. Some citizens pretend to be what they are not and mimic chemicals that others seek out. Some citizens simply block lawful citizens from the legal commerce they seek out, blocking a needed chemical-interaction, from occurring. Undisciplined, rambling thoughts change your brain chemistry, which changes your body chemistry, which changes your thoughts, which cycles back around until you stop the chemistry cycle thought roller-coaster you are stuck on.

SURVIVAL BASED INFORMATION

Using biochemistry, some neuroscientists have proven that utilizing a simple protein inhibitor, they were able to erase a "fear-memory." Your casual-harmless memory reflections upon your past, are not only adaptive, but your brain's cellular representation and neural circuitry is changed every time—what experts call your "natural updating mechanisms." Accessing new information on a specific incident almost always establishes a memory update (contamination) of previous memories? With or without your consent or awareness. You may accidentally retraumatize yourself. Associated **self-protection memories** and emotions may be disturbed, instead of improving later behavioral responses. States of hyperarousal can become habitual, even addictive. Do you modify your own memories, or do you rely on experts or psycho-pharmacy? There are experts involved with the medicine of "molecular-memory." Police-officers routinely deal with internal signals of "unconscious awareness" that escape conscious recognition. A police-officer misperceiving the world, will not truly be aware of complicated situations we find ourselves responding to and projected into—responding with diminished capacity for de-escalation success. What negative thoughts do you keep alive and rooted for unwanted and immediate access in your mind? Scientists have proven that trauma in mice can be "**generationally transmitted**" to their off-spring—up to 5 generations. No wonder that some police-officers re-energize and re-transmit their own

150

trauma back to themselves, or even other police-officers and citizens without conscious deliberation. What I unconsciously categorize as "survival-based-information" may exceed what you consider survival-based information based on your personal history and background. Rupert Sheldrake's theories of "**morphic resonance**," considered controversial, offers information relatable to routine-patrol. Research memory "engrams" to help you understand what imprints (physical/chemical) that your traumatic memories have left behind. Well intended "psychological debriefings" for law-enforcement or military personnel, rarely prevents PTSD. Psychological emotional awareness on your part, is a good first step.

To effectively and efficiently face the negative parts of yourself, you first have to acknowledge the negative parts. It is even harder to admit when you purposefully avoid certain negative parts and never face particular inner-demons. "**Socially based emotions**" as a signal to others what their "internal-world" has them feeling, also as a signal for our own self-analysis of what we are feeling. Police become experts at recognizing "postural-expressions" immediately upon arrival, influencing our citizen interaction—procedural memory impulses. Sometimes when we are planning a future event, we already begin (inner-prompting) attaching negative emotionally stained belief structures, almost guaranteeing failure. Your impatience when dealing with certain citizens usually tells you more about yourself than the citizens we interact with. We are reminded that observing and thinking are two different mental processes. Self-importance and emotional reaction are added to observation skills, and are not a function of observation. Many religious traditions encourage you to "free-your-mind" utilizing attention and focus. It is never too late to start. If, after ten years of policing, you realize that you are only the personality of a police-officer, you have no off-duty non-police personality or identity; self-importance will become your default-status position poison. Your habitual perspective, cognitive preferences, state of existence or your default mode of interpretation, judgement and expression—is how you self-programmed. What you consider freedom, may threaten others in your professional and personal life. Do any of your "personal-value-systems" overrule department guidelines and rules? Must you alter your behavior based on the expectations of other police-officers. How about "cultural-norms." Does compassion always slow down time-sensitive decision-making complex social reasoning skills? Research the *"Forer effect"* to help understand how your unconscious seeks "subjective-validation," out of your awareness. A police-officers search for patterns and meaning will be heavily influenced by the Forer effect. <u>Your cognitive processes are not all conscious and within your awareness</u>.

"Humans are a social-species. Human interpersonal relationships are biologically wired into our very nature. Most of us are neuronally fine-tuned, as a basic social-integrated function, into developing interpersonal relationships. We are culturally prescribed social creatures with socially evolved circuitry and mirror neurons operating from a socially based point-of-view that alters and modifies our behavior. Meaningful and loving social relationships have evolved to require a standing army of law-enforcement officers to maintain civilized order. Socio-cultural architecture also programs and structures your demonization of other cultures. Without interaction between cultures, we can never be proven wrong." From *POLICING PRIVATE PERSONALITIES* Sam Luckey

EMOTIONS AS INTERFACE BETWEEN MIND AND BODY

Behavior profiling. Interpersonal skills. Turning a "citizen-interaction" into a "citizen-confrontation" and a guaranteed arrest. Over-aggressiveness. Burned-out. More police-officers report leaving law-enforcement because of "department-initiated-stressors" (supervisory-department policies), than actual citizen-interaction. Cognitive tunnel vision. Coping mechanisms. Always continue your education. Authority over authoritarian. Learning from experience. Mistakes made while "confident" appear "confident." We freely share with other police-officers our **"subjective experience,"** just the physical pains that happen when you have to wrestle someone into handcuffs. We usually choose not to report those same physical issues, especially mental issues, with medical professionals. "Surrendering" is usually considered in context to "citizens" we interact with. Martial artists who finally find a sensei or instructor that is so expert in their style, "surrender" to the principles of mastery promoted, encouraged and modeled by that same teacher. Law-enforcement needs to surrender to the actual reality of the situation they responded to—present with presence. Not the scene we wanted it to be. We are "set-in-our-ways" and need to solve (consensus) everything within our subjective "time" preferences, wishing for better weather conditions, while experiencing never-ending social-interference. Sometimes, just being in a "group," especially law-enforcement, actually discourages, hinders or punishes **group-think "dissent."** If you disagree with the ambiguous "consensus," you may feel pressured to keep your dissent quiet. Police group-think involves "survival" issues that strike each officer personally with distinct "associated" mental-images that may or may not even be related to the discussion. What you consider "super-stimuli," may be unimportant outside-stimuli to other officers. Anger is used by some of us, even police-officers, as "bargaining-interaction" tools. The **"physiology-of-perception,"** is not tamper-proof, nor resistant to illusion, delusion, or intentional mis-manipulation. Is "perceptual-residue" a real "contradiction."

"First-impressions" that a police-officer initially makes, generally become ambiguous poorly defined judgments, that unconsciously alter a police-officers behavior. **Your emotions become thoughts!** Then we mandate the "burden-of-proof" on the citizen to prove he or she is not the exact replica of our first-impression. *"Affect-heuristic"* may be how most police-officers immediately and unconsciously assess their expectations during this particular citizen-interaction—this person is going to be disorderly, defiant, always interrupting, not hearing what you say, is not a good person and should be dealt with forcefully! Your **associative mental processes** influencing your mood, will contaminate and automatically associate "problems" and conclusions that may not be related. Neuroscientists remind us that our rational methodical mind is neuronally-speaking, very-very slow, when compared to your instinctive emotional mind. Evolutionarily designed survival mental processes, especially when confronted by novel outside-stimuli, need immediate deciphering and optimal behavioral options be provided. You will always be under the influence of the risk/reward feelings your unconscious triggers. Learn to recognize these unconscious feelings before your behavioral response gets you into trouble. **Risk-assessment** is not just visual, you have a whole symphony of "emotion-generating structures" in your brain that leads to your "risk-feelings" awareness and subsequent behavioral responses.

"Have you ever evaluated your personal 'properties-of-behavior' in life-or-death situations? We are experts at detecting patterns that may not really be physically present—especially when determining "meaning" associated or inferred with movement. Most of our "judgments" are made unconsciously. We develop and attach "meaning" to everything we interact with. Everything we have already experienced and expect or anticipate to interact with—is unconsciously neuronally empowered to influence the present moment." From POLICING PRIVATE PERSONALITIES Sam Luckey

DECISION-MAKING EMOTIONAL ASSESSMENTS

Before police-officers' radio in their arrival at a complicated incident, we are already problem-solving internally, using nonconscious biasing, pre-programming and declarative knowledge. We problem-solve and develop pattern recognition before we are even aware of it. Then we start actual conscious deliberative thinking. Your unconscious may be screaming watch out or "that's him," but your conscious deliberation has distracted you into a dangerous situation. Neuroscientists have proven that your decision-making skills require "**emotional-assessment**." After hundreds of years of humans trying to temper their emotional displays, it turned out that decision-making requires an emotional flavoring. Even "simple-choices" require a functional emotional brain in a community of hidden persuasion. If you can imagine or intuit the slightest "benefit" hope or familiarity, the risk interpretation will be lowered. Unconscious mental forces determined "less-risk" when considering behavior options. Under the influence of social cohesion and the "third-person effect," difficulty increases with group size, decreasing most of our self-actualization success-intentions—influencing your "sense-of-self," self-esteem, or self-delusion. A police-officer involved in citizen-interaction from the cognitive viewpoint of "**illusory-superiority-effect**," will eventually be brought back-down-to earth. Ignoring or intentionally forgetting your citizen-interaction "failures," is a form of lying to yourself, your community and your police-in-group. Robert Orstein reports that we are deluded if we believe we are "consistent" and "single-minded" or that you have an actual "real-self!" Emotions have been described as your body's "reaction to your mind." Emotions as the interface between mind and body. Have you ever experienced an emotion without accompanying thoughts? Emotions as "social-constructions" and "intention-signals" for the outside world, appear to be both "innate" and "acquired." Dispositions can become more complicated "neurochemical-states" similar to moods. Neural events that become slightly different more enhanced neural events.

Sometimes, especially in law-enforcement, while in the community, we feel our self-image self-awareness, as if everyone is directing their attention our way—the *"spotlight-effect."* Hyper-awareness of human-observation directed at us, can be good; but it can also distract you into unsafe police-behavior. According to experts, venting our anger may feel good; but in the long-run they claim it primes your future behavior in negative and increasingly aggressive ways—with clinical investigations detecting a "desire-for-vengeance." Would you complain about a mandatory class on not venting anger, but determining your personal healing *"catharsis"* programming? Something you could do as soon as it is safe at any incident that has gotten you aggravated? **Venting your anger** is considered "druglike," in that different brain-chemicals are released when venting, as compared to a cathartic experience. Quitting venting-anger may be a habit you cannot quit. This druglike euphoria while venting could be the reason you actually prefer venting over catharsis. You will still have to deal with the emotions your **emotional library** empowered originally.

"Emotions of a social-basis can also be activated by a stimulus that is no longer present or no longer exists—which makes explaining your behavior to the police, embarrassing. Negative uncontrolled self-talk as a form of disease, easily infecting those around you, as their negative self-talk infects your behavior. Your control over 'thoughts-about-thoughts' cannot just create a new brain state by altering brain chemistry, but can also create a better overall police-officer by changing behavioral outcomes." From POLICING PRIVATE PERSONALITIES Sam Luckey

OLD-BEHAVIORS HABITUALLY RETURN

Many times, in a single shift, police-officers will have their emotional maturity tested over-and-over, without the time to heal before the next dispatch. Some officers have become dependent on venting their anger, in public or out-of-view! Your memories of an incident can be altered (conformity) just by the wording of your inquiry—memories contaminated with your imagination filter. Your police-culture will "social-contagion" the stories (or police-reports) that we document and tell others as part of our normal unconscious survival instincts. It usually only takes 3 or more police-officers to gain your compliancy and convince you to alter statements and documentation. We more easily believe we can defend our honor and truthiness, when confronted by only one or two fellow equal-rank police-officers. We have to fight our normal search for "social-acceptance," when confronted with dubious and illegal influence, because we want to be accepted by other police-officers—**manufactured conformity**. Punishment, or reward for conformity is unconsciously analyzed, first. Whatever pops up into your conscious awareness first, does not guarantee the best behavioral option. "*Classical-conditioning*" in law-enforcement, our search for meaning and expectation, may entrap you in behavior you are not proud of. Your original naive rookie expectations and inclinations, can be soured as the result of "*operant-conditioning;*" that has changed your inclinations and desires—reinforced under the threat or potential for punishment. <u>Old behaviors habitually return</u>, not the good kind.

"*Neuroscientist Michael Gazzaniga warns us that we have 'multiple-mental-systems" that 'produce-behavior' independent of each other. Multiple mental systems" that also initiate 'impulses for action' with no guarantee that the impulses and behavior are what your 'sense-of-self' really intended. Modern human 'circular-causality' seems to prove that 'self-directs-attention' and 'attention determines the self.'" From POLICING PRIVATE PERSONALITIES Sam Luckey.*

Your crime-scene law-enforcement experience occurs as a "process," and only has to relate to what is exactly occurring. All movement occurs as a "process." A "result" is still just a "process." "Process" is not a thing. Goal as "result" is not purpose. What is the purpose/reason for this citizen-interaction? Without a clearly defined purpose, you can't initiate what is appropriate. That's all. Purpose, alignment, strategy, objectives, skill, convictions, interpretation, perspective, timing, personal responsibility, making distinctions, potential options, abilities, habits, intentions. Interpreting an emotion is different than the emotion itself. What emotion(s) do you routinely project? Interactions with emotional citizens routinely infect law-enforcement (**circular-causality**). Is it really the environment that creates your emotional over-reaction? If that is what you believe, then you will not even recognize yourself (perspective) as the cause. A mind that is focused on finding reason to "take-offense"' will succeed in that mission—at the expense of family, employment and friends. A "take-offense" mindset will always create that experience—in a circular feed-back loop—that expectational-bias guaranteed your incoming perception interpretation will always find and verify. A **"take-offense"** personality, if allowed to continue, will become your "**default-predictive-filters**," self-justified by your biased and self-manipulated memories as your only proof. How many of your "patterns-of-behavior" are really just reflection of the "identity" you carry—what others have labeled, categorized or trapped you in? Are you behaving as others expect, rather than what you would really prefer. Has your personal identity or public personal been trained, conditioned, or replaced by others without your consent or even awareness? "Selfhood, or personal and public empowered identity, as a filter that can remove you from the here and now.

CITIZEN INTERACTION—ACTIVITY AS RELATIONSHIP

While training "rookies," I emphasized an aspect of "responses" and "reactions" that most never consider. When a rookie seems a little overzealous or more authoritarian over minor incidents, I remind them to experience these "responses" and "reactions" as a "behavior," instead of something that just-happened-to-them or at-them. You were not an object without intention, you were "behavior," action-behavior, personal, and responsible for that "behavior." Responding and reacting behavioral responses carry "limits" so demanding, that you won't even be aware that there are other more positive responses and reactions at your fingertips. When you are calm, confident and slightly alert in your "response" to an incident, the chances of a successful resolution increases. When you fall into "reactivity" instead, automatic impulses, good or bad, happen faster than you can retract them. Respond with dignity and fairness instead. Your "relationship" during citizen-interaction is not an object—it is an "activity." It is a job requirement and you are duty-bound to perform to the best of your unbiased ability. Law-enforcement is your "field-of-interaction." Do not let "future projections" distract you from what is happening right before your eyes (here-and-now). Well-intentioned assumptions and conclusions can also entrap you or distract you from needed corrections or even recognizing that a change in plans or course is needed. Law-enforcement connecting with what is really happening, not what they would like to happen. Are the "bad-guys" leading you to where they want you to be, while your distracted by thoughts of future experiences? Are you content with random success, rather than consistent success. MASH star Alan Alda wrote a book called "If I Understood You, Would I have This Look on my face?" A reviewer identified the following theme that the book encourages: "To become a better communicator you must understand what other people are thinking. You must put yourself in the shoes of your audience and develop empathy." If years in law-enforcement have you only hanging around other law-enforcement officers, only thinking police thoughts all the time and feeling trapped in only law-enforcement interpretation modes of thought and expression—this book is a start for you to regain a healthier community mindset.

Detecting "depression" issues in law-enforcement co-workers can be rather difficult. There can be many-diverse reasons behind depression (considered a syndrome or spectrum by some authors/scientist), for law-enforcement. We are exposed to the worst society has to offer, the worst violent crime scenes, routinely feeling our hands are tied in our official "legal" choices and options while on patrol. Associated symptoms and characteristics of depression, especially in law-enforcement, seem to contradict with opposite experiences and impairment. The short adrenaline rush of a physical takedown or felony arrest, can appear to others as the opposite of "depression." Many law-enforcement officers still fear revealing any depression or psychological disturbances to their supervisors, even their own spouses. "**Treatment-resistant-depression**" is a real thing. Clinical investigations into depression have revealed that patients with similar symptoms of depression and similar severity, will frequently show brain activity scans that are not similar. Doctors have perfected a method of "<u>fecal-transplant</u>" that can make someone depressed if the fecal matter was from a depressed patient. We now have "healing fecal-transplants" routinely across America, donated by healthy "normal" biological humans. Depression may be caused by your "default-mode-network" malfunctioning. Your depression may be caused by your "**patterns-of-reactivity**" towards all the emotional stimulus that you are required to confront. Your "rewarding stimuli" interpretations may have changed since your rookie years. Have you ever evaluated and confronted your own personal "brain-activation-patterns?" As complicated as mind/brain/body interaction is, it is even more complicated to verify "neural-markers" that identify exactly what is really happening in each of us. Back when I was a patrolman, I relished the "hunt" when chasing vehicles who refused to stop. Now, in my 60's, I watch chase YouTube videos and realize I no longer have the patience or even discipline for such chases, even though I feel so much more mature and disciplined now, than when I was a hyper-active much younger Army MP on multiple overseas tours. I am alarmed at how much anger I feel at these drivers—just watching the YouTube

160

video! It is not any fear related to potential vehicle accidents during the chase, it is my worry that I would illegally be judge, jury and executioner. My deepest respect to those officers who remain so calm and patient when the driver is finally apprehended.

When the national news reports a **"Critical Incident,"** most citizens identify the "critical" part to be referring to the citizens that may be involved. Most law-enforcement departments identify the critical part as referring to the potential danger to an officer's mental health and physical safety. Most police-officers have a reality-based analysis of their own strengths and weaknesses. If we are going to have a problem emotionally or physically with what we are racing to, we are usually **self-talked into awareness and prepare our "self."** A small percentage either overestimate their skills and usefulness, or underestimate a negative self-image. Supervisors at these critical incidents need to be supervisors more than friends of other responding officers at that moment. Rushed responses to dangerous incidents utilize more unconscious concept and categorization skills, than conscious evaluation. Supervisors need to know their team. What individual specific personal problems are each of your team members solving on their own? Can you help? Should you help? For some reason, offering to help someone, occasionally turns into a disastrous misinterpretation and long uncomfortable moments. Most of our interactions with citizens lacks the benefit of analysis concerning their past behavior as a means to predict their future behavior. I would like to believe that *"social-loafing,"* where participation in group-effort, results in most participants, unconsciously motivate less effort and work on behalf of the group, than, if they were on their own; does not apply to law-enforcement. An incident back in the late 1980's proved "social-loafing" can occur in law-enforcement. About ten correctional-officers took a bus from our facility in Northwest Indiana, to a Chicago White Sox game. After the game, we all joined the crowd heading back to the parking lot, when a uniformed Chicago Police officer started screaming profanities at everybody to stick to the overcrowded sidewalks, and get out of the street. There were no vehicles allowed on this street during the game, so that is where the crowd was innocently pushed into. This Chicago Police officer was cussing at everyone, even little kids. Our senior member, afterwards, contacted this officer's supervisor to complain. Turned out that officer had been pulled from road-duty, to a desk job years ago, because he was so horrible a police-officer, but his union kept him from being fired. This officer was just pissed that he was forced to work law-enforcement temporarily again. This officer, out in the public, had no *"evaluation-apprehension"* at all!

BEYOND VERBALLY ACCESSIBLE MEMORIES

Psychological casualties. Police psychologist Laurence Miller reports that, "The goal of **crisis intervention** is stabilization for later treatment," not necessarily therapy. Crisis prevention before crisis intervention. "Traumatic memories" influence police behavior, even if we are unaware of these traumatic memories. After a traumatic event, you might experience the *"Illusion of Transparency,"* where you believe "others" can decipher your private thoughts or emotional fluctuation. Your private inner turmoil is naturally felt as more intense within; unless you initiate inappropriate (outward) observable behavior based on your inner-turmoil. Experts insist that for the healing to begin, we need to go beyond "verbally accessible memory." Undisciplined thought processes begin within, especially when self-awareness spends so much time imagining what other people are privately thinking within. It may be easier to begin the healing process by working with your "explicit memory," but, experts stress that **"implicit memory"** is just as important; but much, much harder to clearly identify. Most police-officers develop the belief that they can detect liars a mile away, but are not much better at detecting liars than regular citizens. Out on the streets, focusing on your own mental state is not where self-pity, angry self-analysis and self-awareness should be conducted. We may feel our "destiny" expectations are not being met—surrendering to futility, or worse, a mental automatic shutdown.

"Your 'beliefs-as-programming,' make your subsequent behavior seem normal and appropriate, because your mind is content when your behavior matches your belief programming, 'coherence' as one author described it. When you respond to an incident what 'belief-systems' are you promoting, defending, energizing, dragging along or using as a 'shield' or barrier between you and the public. Human neural architecture has 'systems' and 'systems-of-systems' Belief systems are not always positive influences on the individual, society or culture." From POLICING PRIVATE PERSONALITIES, Sam Luckey.

PERCEPTUAL ANALYSIS AND TEACHABLE MOMENTS

Police-officers, just like all citizens, auto-interpret their physical sensations into "words-as-substitutions" and metaphors for their feelings. Sometimes the label we give to a "feeling" becomes more important than the actual feeling. The label empowers the "feeling" long after the feeling has dissipated. The label or words you choose infect your perceptions and behavioral response, more than the original "feeling." **Habitual words change your thoughts**. The biggest influence on your current thought is not the outside world, but your previous thought. Everybody can take a few seconds to recognize when they habitually entrap themselves in words that are not appropriate or helpful for de-escalation techniques. Provide yourself a "teachable-moment" and develop a more positive word-choice habit! The words you choose, along with your original perceptive analysis infect your mood more than we would like to admit—the *"anchoring effect."* Your decision-making processes are usually anchored in the *anchoring-effect*. Bias and anchoring influence your attention skills and perceptive analysis. We may be part of a "paramilitary organization," but, with open minds we can be so much more. Police anticipating and averting potential citizen conflicts. If the conflict has already started, initiate intervention.

Patrol-supervisors can develop short ten-minute training sessions provided on a regular basis as a form of "stress-management."

"Abstract concepts 'determine-our-experience' more than we are aware of. What we 'sense' are not 'certainties.' Assumptions and inferences infect our interpretations of every interaction we have and every belief we hold. Recognize when secondary processes (cognition and emotional elements) interfere with your primary experience of the world. Is it the world that you are upset with or your own mental interpretation that is creating the disconnect.?"

PERSONALITY, MEMORIES AND PSYCHOLOGIAL TENDENCIES

Developing a sincere interest in the community you patrol decreases unplanned physical-force moments, over de-escalation techniques. Sometimes, a police-officer that has nothing to do with a citizen's complaint, can de-escalate an incident, by just letting a noncompliant upset citizen, vent and vent and vent. Instead of an arrest report, we can just make a small entry in our patrol-log. "How-to-police" is a different skill-set than understanding rules, regulations and the law, especially **"how to get along with other police-officers."** A citizen just watching me write down most of what they "yelled," seems to calm them down. Repeating back to the citizen their complaints is almost as good as writing down what they say. Getting the citizen to focus (attending skills) on the key-issues involving their law-enforcement interaction is a good first step. A citizens first police encounter will shape their attitude towards all future police encounters. A police-officers "inborn-preferences," if left unchecked and unanalyzed, unconscious bias and preferences will become more basic to your exposed to others, personality. There is a respected psychological analysis used on law-enforcement that breaks down police-officers to variations of four types of influence on your judgment. Thinking/Feeling/Sensing/Intuition. **We investigate the unknown by using the known.** The next time you are required to approach a potentially violent citizen, remember that his personality only consists of "memories and psychological tendencies."

"We are dispatched to a situation, perceive, interpret 'stimulus,' experience physiological changes in our bodies, which create interpretive mood dances—based more on unconscious dispositions. These dispositions influence your personal attitude directed at the citizens you responded to assist, infecting their emotions and feelings, which continue infecting your emotions and feeling, in perpetual circular-feedback and on-and-on. Everyone processing information in their brain according to their own self-serving prioritized goals and objectives." From POLICING PRIVATE PERSONALITIES, Sam Luckey

TUNNEL VISION/CHANGE BLINDNESS/PERCEPTUAL BLINDNESS

The faster we respond in a patrol-car, the more **"tunnel-vision"** will affect our vision and memories. We would like to believe we never patrol or interact with citizens under the influence of tunnel-vision. Our attention and awareness skills actually require tunnel-vision selective processing. Otherwise, we would be overwhelmed by everything in our vision-field. Expectations and intentional focus require tunnel-vision on what we need to be focused on, blurring what we accept or expect to be not important. No need for our attention. **Inattentional blindness** leads to false-judgements, summaries and poor perception skills. Your *neuronal simulation-stimulation-situation* is always an edited version of reality. It is up to you to recognize the differences. Some citizens are experts at creating "misdirection;" making distracted or unaware police-officers embarrassingly fall for their intended "perceptual-blindness." Fully engaged in tunnel-vision attentional processing on one aspect of your outside-stimuli analysis—can more easily make you miss something out of your tunnel-vison awareness that may be important. Even "context" determined at this particular incident, especially <u>false-safety interpretations</u>, may make you more vulnerable to *"change-blindness"* and *"inattentional-blindness."* You may even motivate false-beliefs incompatible with just what you responded to.

"Inner motivations are easy to hide from 'others,' because most of us are not even aware that we have 'unconscious motivations,' 'unconscious expectations,' unconscious judgments,' and 'unconscious assumptions and beliefs.' It is easy to effortlessly hide mental context concepts and unconscious behavior inclination patterns and dispositions you do not know you have. We all have brain forces functioning independent of conscious control. Sometimes the evil and devious side of motivational behavior can be—behaviorally invisible, therefore behaviorally immeasurable— until it is revealed for what it is." From POLICING PRIVATE PERSONALITIES, Sam Luckey.

Make sure your non-verbal behavior reflects what you verbalize to the citizen. If they suspect deception, it may be based on an unconscious interpretation of the police-officers non-verbal behavior. At emotional incidents, the unconscious rules the conscious. **"Ambiguity tolerance"** is not just a key hostage-negotiation skill, it is also vital for everybody in law-enforcement. There have been about two dozen incidents of a police-officer taking hostages in recent decades. One incident was reported that the hostage-taker was not only a police-officer, but a trained hostage negotiator himself. I was fortunately to attend an FBI Hostage Negotiation course in West Germany. Two excellent instructors, one of whom was an Army MP reservist, a Colonel. We were chasing Libyan hit squads across Europe, while at the same time, beefing up security for all VIPs that CID was responsible for their security. It was cheaper to send two FBI trainers to West Germany, than send 20+ CID Agents to the U.S. A hostage situation committed by a law-enforcement officer may have been initiated because he could not commit to **"committing suicide,"** and may be hoping for an "officer-initiated-shooting" form of suicide." Well-meaning mental-health initiatives have almost guaranteed that if you admit to a co-worker, human-resources or law-enforcement that you have considered suicide, you may be involuntarily admitted to a mental-health facility if your fortunate, or usually, a large county jail not designed for such a patient. Many police departments started at a time where "robber barons" and the rich focused them on taking out labor-union activists, instead of fighting crime. Many of the "drug-crimes" that we spend so much time targeting and investigating, are really just **"prohibition"** crimes meant to distract us from legal prescription drug abuse, alcohol and tobacco. A "free-society" that protects the rights of alcohol and tobacco producers (commerce first). Buddhist tradition encourages using your attention skills to **cultivate compassion**. If you, especially as a police-officer, operate primarily from a distracted default-mode-network, compassion will escape your mental processes. It is your professional purpose to merge your police-sciences mechanistic view of the world, with your personal "wholistic" experience and job performance.

SELF-HANDICAPPING REALITY NEGOTIATION

Is the diagnosis of **"personality disorder,"** culturally determined by outsiders based simply on "deviation" from socio-cultural expected norms? Are determinations of personality "extremes" less science and more at-that-moment determinations, ambiguous and fluctuating? Genius in "abstract thinking" can easily be misdiagnosed as pathology. A diagnosis influenced by someone's "lack-of-empathy," needs to be based on a true understanding of that someone's life. Anticipatory-rationalization may infect some police-officers responding to a complicated incident. Some self-talk themselves in ways that "protect-their-ego;" as a form of reality-negotiation rambling about all the ways "others" may interfere with you solving or de-escalating the incident. Blaming external forces before behavior justifies any blame, is considered "self-handicapping." Self-handicapping can also apply to group-attitudes, especially police-departments with low morale. We create advance "excuses" meant to protect our fragile-ego. Military veterans become experts when they detect that someone in their unit exhibits a "mood," that may mean they are falsely creating self-handicapping excuses concerning a mission about to be embarked on. We were advised that actually "sad" soldiers were just being more honest with themselves about their feelings, especially self-worth. Human interaction may have some basic socio-cultural expectations and obligations, but simply dropping out-of-life may simply mean giving yourself more time to write without interference—like me.

"Have your stimulus-response patterns been exploited by socially-conditioned indoctrination—without your awareness and permission? Most of us are limited to only experience and display emotions (intensity and duration) we already have on file as personal 'pre-existing programs of emotion.' Something sets off a certain emotional display, with or without cognitive conscious consent, and we rarely question why? We judge ourselves 'justified,' even if the emotional display was counter-productive or inappropriate for the reality of the situation. Future consequences are not considered or evaluated." From POLICING PRIVATE PERSONALITIES, Sam Luckey

I enjoyed Stephanie Dowrick's book, "Seeking the Sacred, Transforming our View of Ourselves and One Another." She discusses our spiritual searching "freedom-of-inquiry" (from experts in the spiritual/religious field), who we assign the trait of "reverence." She is open-minded and accepting of my spirituality over religion belief systems. Reading her book, I realized that most police-officers accepted or energized attitudes of reverence from the community. Her example was intended for religious related interaction, but she used attributes of "self-importance," "sentimentality," and "portentousness," that can be **mistaken for "reverence".** All three easily transfer to law-enforcement interaction and interpretation, out in the community. Challenging the interference of negative traits, transformation requires actually doing something, made harder, because you have to admit you have a negative trait requiring self-neuroplasticity that won't cost you any money at all. Heal thyself—before you are the last person in your lifetime to die! The one "infidel" that you never challenged was "thyself." Law-enforcement is susceptible to the "labeling-theory" in a bidirectional process. We "label" citizens we are about to interact with, while the citizen labels us. A police-officer present at a violent crime scene, is not really present; if their thoughts are trapped in past interactions that have nothing to do with the incident you responded to. At the scene of a violent incident, everybody who responded is trying to understand and **predict the behaviors** of everybody present; victim, witness, subjects and other police-officers. Our here/now present analysis will lead to rushed assumptions that create behavioral responses. Sometimes we guess right, and sometimes wrong. Experts warn us that *"Self-Fulfilling Prophecies"* and other false interpretations can spread like a social-contagion to others involved, or just nearby—actually artificially creating the false future as a self-fulfilled prophetic reality, becoming a **"vacillating consensus of beliefs."** Not good for law-enforcement.

SOCIAL-MASK INTERACTION FILTERS

Most modern law-enforcement agencies contract out some sort of **"personality-profiling"** for applicants and current members. Most of us utilize "sensing and intuitive" aspects of routine-patrol visual analysis from a more unconscious aspect. Whatever aspect, sensing or intuitive, that bubbles up into our conscious awareness, just seems right for that moment. A distracted, depressed or angry and uncaring police-officer is actually surrendering to the "hope" that he or she outwits or *"outsmarts-random-chance"* till end-of-shift! The ***"illusion-of-control"*** can get you killed. *"Learned-helplessness"* can get you killed. Do not patrol in a mood that simply means patrolling while "coexisting-with-chaos." We spend our shifts seeking pattern recognition signals that may-or-may-not be simple random noise. The answers we provide to personality-profiling questionnaires, are usually censored with or without our awareness. We were evolutionarily designed **to filter our interactions** with strangers utilizing subjective expectations about their "personality" and character—considered a shortcut to cognition. This is normally an effortless mental process performed out of our awareness. The filtered on-the-spot by you-conclusion; will be how your first instinct or intuition about the person, became your default mode of interaction—the *"social-mask"* you created for the citizen in question, right or wrong. Bias and prejudice can influence your opinion of the individual; ignoring "situational" aspects of their dilemma, and primarily blaming their "personality" or "disposition."

"Human neural system communication in the form of 'signals' or 'integrated representations,' utilize 'feedforward projections,' 'feedback projections,' reciprocal feedback projections,' and 'reciprocal projection backward.' All this to create an image in your mind. Remember the 'image' in your mind is not just visual. During violent emotional incidents, it may be possible that your brain is confusing your behavior with the other's behavior. What could go wrong?" From POLICING PRIVATE PERSONALITIES, Sam Luckey

We auto-anticipate clues in our environment, as we step deeper and deeper into the situation we responded to. We don't hesitate to recognize **"set-and-setting,"** the environment, and the "power-of-the-situation, when police-officers get themselves into serious trouble—while not giving citizens the same consideration. If we were (not police-officers), simply a citizen living in the same areas we find "difficult," we would also prefer leaving our house with weapons, legally or illegally! Conscious control still requires primitive mind/brain processes working within our more advanced and newer mind/brain processes. We rarely have time to determine "consistency," in our interpretation of the citizen's behavior. Have you ever taken the time to investigate your skills in decision-making? Has a supervisor ever questioned your decision-making skills? How rational are your judgments? Emotional impulses empowered by your emotional library, influence your rationality, more than we would like to believe. **"Feeling" based decisions** are tempered by your cortex. All your mental analysis, context assessment and categorization, creates emotional flavoring awareness—feelings as summaries of your private emotional data at that moment. A confident, well-trained and experienced veteran police-officer easily and effortlessly determines "which "mode-of-thought" will work best for the situation they responded to. That is how we were designed. We have the power to decline our initial intuition and instincts, if more information identifies different routes and methodology. Reason, oddly requires emotional influence for accurate and healthy decision-making.

"While working a horrible emotionally violent shift, we may be over-stimulated to the point we no longer process everything we witness and experience. This is when unconscious beliefs and intentions seem to confirm what we are told; if, that confirms what we already believe without conscious contradictive investigative analysis. 'Enculturation' may bypass the human gift of 'full heart-brain-mind dialogue.' Witnessing attitudes that become 'personalities-of-attitude.'" From POLICING PRIVATE PERSONALITIES Sam Luckey

EXPECTATIONS CHANGE YOUR EXPERIENCE

Our mammal brain is not concerned initially about accuracy; only **immediate and automatic categoric** effort originally designed to detect quickly, dangerous or "novel" individuals. We will then always welcome "information" about that person that supports our auto-mental-model we initially categorized the individual in—until more information changes our initial estimation of the person in question. I like author Jonah Lehrer's quote: **"A brain that can't**

feel, can't make up its mind." Philosopher David Hume said that, "reason was the slave of the passions." We will more easily accept as "truth," negativities about the person in question, if these negativities match the mental model we initially determined—considered "*representativeness heuristics*." Your expectations about the individual have not only been altered, but also narrowed into a "belief" that may not match the reality of the individual in question. The citizen's behavior that triggered your attention; may be categorized by your initial determination concerning "disposition" expectations, flavored by the social-situation—potential "attribution-errors." Law-enforcement is highly susceptible to **"contaminated" awareness and attention**; meaning that you were directed or misdirected into someone else's preference and judgments, before self-analysis can be safely and thoroughly conducted. Expectations change your experience, especially decision-making and safety issues, sometimes more than the actual situation.

"*Perception seems more immediate (meaning-determination), while consciousness can reflect on the 'qualitative characteristics' of what we perceive. Your perceptions can be altered when accompanied by thoughts based only from unconscious and unverified beliefs and expectations. Assessing the present situation to create a future situation, over-and-over. Your genes metabolize your experience. You may mistake your 'thoughts' as reflective of 'reality,' but your thoughts are not anybody else's reality.*" From POLICING PRIVATE PERSONALITIES Sam Luckey

SOCIAL-SELVES COGNITIVE DISSONANCE

During a complicated and violent incident, we usually have no choice but to immediately respond to orders and directions before we have time to determine the accuracy or intent behind those orders and directions. Our personal definitions determining what aspects of law-enforcement are influenced by your sensing self over your intuitive self, are not clearly determined, and usually intermix in certain socio-cultural aspects. Your **"sense-of-self"** is not a concrete defined personality, only a "sense." You have interaction in your head between a "self" that is current here/now, and a "self" considered the **"remembering-self.**" The remembering self is the one that usually makes your decisions for you. This makes consistent and appropriate behavior, harder. William James recognized a long time ago, that you have "as many different social selves as there are distinct groups of persons about whose opinion you care about," potentially creating cognitive dissonance. Do you consider yourself "dependable?" Some personality-profiling indicates that your job happiness may be more determined by your skills at sensing or intuiting. You may be more upset with the administrative aspects of law-enforcement, instead of the normal routine difficulties of being a peace-officer" in a community that doesn't like law-enforcement in their neighborhood.

"Our mind allows 'the perceptions of others' to not just be mentally considered as described, but these perceptions of others can be 'hardwired into our brains,' as if we had taken the time to verify them, which we hardly ever really do. Some of us utilize a mind that is more of a 'foreign-installation,' than self-created, self-empowered, understood, verified, maintained and empowered." From POLICING PRIVATE PERSONALITIES Sam Luckey

Larger law-enforcement organizations recognize that the success of a police-trainer riding along with new-officers, can be negatively influenced if the "trainer" and the "rookie" have incompatible **"teaching-styles"** and **"learning-styles."** How often do we consider the same potential differences when we are trying to de-escalate something in the community—incompatible differences between police-officer and citizen. The citizen may also have different "learning-styles" incompatible with your "teaching" or de-escalating styles. Occasionally, at an emotionally violent and stressful incident, you realize that it all started because someone energized a small incident into the land of "take-offense" and labels. Just because someone offered a well-meaning alternative or minor deviation—sets off something primal in another person. Sometimes the solution offered by law-enforcement, sets off both or all parties involved. Take responsibility for your "words and actions" when they do not improve the situation. No journey required. You already possess what you need to take responsibility. How inconsistent, arbitrary and unstable are your police responses? **You are "influenced" and also the "influencer."** Your thoughts and perceptions create the world that you respond to and interact with. Are you the bully that because he was getting no attention, learned that the "fear" of others was more preferable to being invisible? Is "restraint" in your personal dictionary? Just because the community we patrol cycles through harm and retaliation, does not mean we also have to. If you have no idea who you would like to become, you will not recognize when you stray from or hinder your dreams. You are always more than what has happened to and at you, stop prolonging your feelings of intolerance, "suffering" and being wronged. It is not uncommon for someone to initially, feel better about themselves, because they abused and wronged another.

"An emotion producing stimulus may trigger an automatic 'conditioned-emotional-response' (programming) based simply on past 'emotional-learning' response skills, or lack of skills. Sometimes a police-officer becomes so fed-up with responding to a particular club, neighborhood or business, that just being dispatched becomes a 'conditioned-stimulus' eliciting personal 'conditioned responses' that hopefully other police officers recognize in you and redirect or prevent questionable police-behavior." From POLICING PRIVATE PERSONALITIES, Sam Luckey

SOCIAL VIOLATIONS AND EMOTIONAL IMPORTANCE

Your experience-conditioned-judgmental-mind, operating undisciplined and fixated on "unconscious cognitive preferential"

habitual-behavioral pre-motor-programming; are harder to recognize if you have never self-analyzed your specific cognitive processing preferences and skills, and truly understand the pre-programming influence of your unconscious. Who programmed you? With your permission? "Cultural social-characteristics" that you unconsciously empower and embolden as facts. "Culturally-inherited" unquestionable social-truths, are typically more obviously recognizably apparent to yourself and your "culture" (emotional-importance), than "others" or outsiders" interpretational recognition—will "we" encourage indoctrinated reasons to be offended by an alleged social-violation interpretational dance of offended—yes, or no? Violence is justified and a proper social-response for the "offended." Clashes of civilization being reinvigorated here in America—especially worldly intractable conflicts believed to be unsolvable. Indoctrinated reasons that do not make any sense to other cultures. Is it actually "improper" to not be offended from within the "offended" culture? Governments world-wide budgetary intentions favor the "science-of-war," over the "science-of-peace," as Raphael Dubois noted before World War I broke out. You may believe yourself to be impeccable, without any racial or cultural bias; falsely interacting in your community without considering the all-important "**context-of-culture**" so important for law-enforcement success. Your well-intended message and verbal skills may be received in a contextual flavor that you did not intend. What are the "indicators" you recognize in de-escalation technique successes, that are shared by multiple de-escalation successes? Share them!

"Culture has been described as a 'set of beliefs and practices,' that Joseph Chilton Pearce further described as 'mutually shared anxiety state.' Describe 'culture' without 'symbolic thought' and 'symbolic language.' What do you have left to describe culture. This highlights the difficulty in preparing our children for their introduction into 'culture.' This also highlights the difficulty for police-officers working

175

in a community of multiple-cultural social-influences." From POLICING PRIVATE PERSONALITIES Sam Luckey

Occasionally, we become **pre-conditioned armed-response-robots**, negatively responding to certain businesses, neighborhoods and even individuals. Then we only perceive and detect what we were conditioned to expect—and unconsciously discard information that runs counter to our emotionally stained unconscious belief system. Sometimes we are so overconfident in our "solution," that we take **disagreement-feedback**, personal, and refuse to even consider a modified solution. We're getting burned out. I found successful de-escalation techniques initiated by veteran police-officers operating from unconscious-programmed "debate" stratagem, and by those utilizing unconscious "dialogue" stratagem. Social roles to be played out in-public, unconsciously energized and structurally determined potential life-altering interaction. Police-citizen interaction from unconscious-pre-programmed debate-stratagem belief systems— auto-robotic cops in action; or novel and empowering original transformation techniques. Successful de-escalation—as intended by unconscious pre-programming. Skills we have, that we are usually unaware of. It's nice when it works. Some of us automatically pre-program our unconscious to displace negative pre-programming images that we subtly recognize lurking in our unconscious impulses and habitual behavior—counter-productive pre-programmed failure—to prove de-escalation techniques do not work! Military and police-intelligence units can gain valuable information just from open-air "public" discussion by and about certain groups of interest. We want to find information documenting "what is there," not what we hoped would be there— pre-programmed unreliable bias.

SECONDARY ARGUMENTS AND DISPUTES

If you were well-trained in "debate" strategy in school (meaning you actually debated numerous times—not just textbook trained), this will infect your de-escalation skills in good ways and bad ways. The "**debate-indoctrinated**" problem-solving police-officer will feel unconsciously empowered (winning!) every time a "flaw" or "defect" is detected concerning citizen-interaction de-escalation; which, is usually disclosed by habitual body-language and facial expressions to the citizen interacted with. Your mind-set has been unconsciously "debate" programmed and "primed" to be the first to prove the other-wrong—or you are a loser. You may be consciously believing you are intending proactive positive de-escalation techniques—while totally unaware your unconscious is in charge and involved in only debate-techniques. Winning debates does not implement de-escalation empowerment. When unconscious pre-programming is in charge of your citizen-interaction, out of your awareness; dialogic debate becomes argument and dispute based oppositional viewpoints that require confusing "**secondary-disputes**" to arise and help-explain further justification qualification verbal-exercises in futility. The more a "debate-trained" police-officer debates a citizen, by normal debate standards; the police-officer is merely affirming his or hers **unconscious-point-of-view**—not intending de-escalation citizen-interaction techniques. Routinely alienating and offending a citizen is debate-acceptable, if you unconsciously believe yourself to be in the right.

"Self-conscious awareness and attention are empowered through the use of language. Do you require language-based thoughts to practice a form of 'mind-control' called 'concentration?' Experts remind us that the words we use do not actually carry meaning. The cognitive experience the receiver interprets of those same words 'evoke-meaning.' To clearly communicate our thinking to others and verify they properly understood our 'meaning,' requires the 'others' to communicate clearly, their thinking back at us. Even 'signs' do not

carry meaning. The receiver/observer 'evokes meaning,' and pattern recognition, a 'construing' interpretation and prediction process."
From *POLICING PRIVATE PERSONALITIES* Sam Luckey

Regardless of what you consciously and physically verbalize, your unconscious point-of-view determines your happiness, frustration, sadness and anger issues, for you or at you. Debate stratagem requires the police-officer to **defend unverified assumptions** while critiquing the citizen—usually in public, which creates more social-dysfunction. Mistakenly believing that we have won a "debate," because we habitually filtered citizen-speak—only seeking to identify weaknesses and flaws in their presentation. It sounds counter-intuitive, but; unconsciously empowered debate stratagem in all our police-interactions—negatively infects **approach and withdrawal behavior**, weapon use justification, personality issues of bias and racism, and pesky emotion and feeling habitual reactions. Debate strategy can distract you from successful de-escalation and even convince you that the "right-answer" existed before you arrived on-scene—and you just have to convince all parties of your wisdom before they have spoken one word to you.

UNCONSCIOUS BEHAVIORAL EXPRESSION

Experts like David Bohm, Frank Boulton and others all seem to identify **"dialogue"** as the more social-agreement positive alternative for "debate." In an "ideal" environment, safety-issues, enough time available, a police-officer can motivate common understanding (all-sides) consensus and collaboration. Occasionally, just having a party that promotes "illogical" beliefs and justifications to be "offended," publicly verbalize their thought processes, helps them realize just how insignificant or mistaken his "mental" injuries really were. Police have to take "mental" injuries (invisible to the naked eye) seriously, because verbal descriptions may differ from the reality of the behavior exhibited. Facial expressions, body language needs and wants, have to be analyzed with what is being

178

said, and even what is not being expressed. Sometimes there is valuable information revealed during **periods of silence**—just watching the citizens eyes and other non-verbal behavior. In my 2nd book, Policing Private Personalities, I describe that after the Vietnam war, MPs like me, responding to disorderly or suspicious behavior, met soldiers displaying no emotions. They just **silently stared at us**, ignoring friendly conversational attempts—de-escalation techniques. One of us would give our .45 to another MP, and volunteer to wrestle the soldier into cuffs and determine if detention or a mental facility was more appropriate. Almost fifty years later, after reading hundreds of books on mental-health issues; I feel that the soldier's conscious-mind, when confronted by MPs, realized they could not consciously explain what their **unconscious programming had them behaviorally expressing**. The last thing an MP would want to do, is shoot a soldier experiencing cognitive dysfunction—the soldier unable to self-explain their behavior that required an MP response.

Dialogue that is not open-minded, is not dialogue. Proper productive **de-escalation dialogue**, easily reveals mistaken counter-productive debate ideology. Who will speak-up? Who habitually becomes "offended" when citizen-interaction de-escalation techniques are steered back to more productive dialogue exercises in connectivity and interdependent social-empowerment. Attitudes and fears are projected requiring correct interpretation by others, made more difficult during police-citizen interaction requiring de-escalation techniques. Do routine criminals become "terrorists," only because their actions run in opposition to governing authorities. Who is experiencing this terrorism "fear-inducing-effect" the strongest; the people or the government. How do we **de-escalate terrorist noncombatants** in a non-violent way, that is not considered brain-washing or re-education camps? Can we keep law-enforcement from being contaminated by anti-terrorist rhetoric and enforcement—that sees de-escalation as a weakness?

CULTURAL AWARENESS PRIORITIES

Undisciplined parents and police-officers usually fail at properly disciplining their children, or are too busy to calmly and effectively de-escalate and positively influence a situation. A well-respected author described the process of "communication," especially involving law-enforcement, as an "art-form." Cultural complex-communication for some ethnic groups, utilize **"silence"** as a way of communicating what is needed to be expressed. We usually misinterpret this "silence" as a negatively intended barrier. Your personal "mental preferences" may not be met or even sabotaged by outside players; how do you respond? Cultural awareness classes are only effective if they are based-in-reality, not well-intended wishful-thinking as a way to say that at least we tried something! Avoiding "hot-topics" may seem effective, but these "hot-topics" should be explored in a way that de-escalates before it is too late. Law-enforcement personal priorities and preferences, seem to be influenced negatively by how busy our shift allows for us to be good "community" police. If we are having a horribly busy shift, we feel justified in limiting our interaction with the community and the energy we provide for de-escalation. You will operate less from a compassionate-heart-based frame-of-reference, and it just seems normal and proper. Recognize that all the newspapers, magazines and TV news that you watch, are not the same "media" that your community may digest.

When I responded as a patrolman to a complicated incident, aware that I would be the only patrol available, I felt more confident and surer of myself. While "infallibility" is a trait that many police-officers energize, it was not one of my traits. Routinely sexually assaulted and beaten by my parents growing up, eliminated any resemblance of overconfidence or infallibility on my part. I did possess normally important "self-reliance" skills, resulting in numerous comments by other patrols, investigators or agents, of: "Why didn't **you call someone for help**?" In the 1970s and 1980s I do not remember ever being psychologically screened. Nowadays, periodic psychological screening is recommended for law-enforcement, possibly even a prerequisite for employment. **Excessive risk-taking** was usually how supervisors described me. I think it was just more going to High School in Gary Indiana during the early 1970s, when Gary was fighting Detroit and Washington D.C. for murder capital of the United States. When you are alone on the streets of Gary and confronted by groups of wannabe and actual gang-members, you have to respond immediately, before their trap is set. That was just how I worked in law-enforcement. The "Sense-of-isolation" that so many fear, was indoctrinated into my psyche when I was a child as a positive-good-feeling. Nobody hurting me when I was alone as a kid. Family "love" was just an "instrument-of-manipulation." I was good at "thinking-outside-the-box," skills beneficial for the patrolman or special agent. I was never the "problem-officer" who responded slowly to dispatches, who never really solved anything or needed supervisory encouragement. I accepted 16-to-20-hour workdays more because I enjoyed the different law-enforcement jobs I held around the world. I took my **"solve-rate"** very seriously, and, even as a patrolman, I would take it personally when I would find out something happened in the area that I patrolled during my shift. Even if it was deep inside a third-floor tanker barracks wall-locker, where I was never allowed to patrol. That would bother me and I would check any sources I have. Rarely, were these in the barracks wall-locker thefts committed by a stranger. Usually someone in the unit, about 20% of the time a good friend of the victim.

EMOTIONAL REFLEX AND SITATIONAL APPRAISAL

It was not until the late 1980s, that neuroscientist experiments highlighted just how much childhood trauma influences not just the child-victim into adulthood, but the **child-victims later own children**. Neuroscientist Michael Meaney developed creative methods that revealed that nurtured and cared for rat pups, "grew

181

into adults that were more laid-back, less reactive to stress, and less prone to addictive behaviors." Imagine if all the "regulars" who attract law-enforcement to their risky behaviors and criminal activity, were more laid-back, less reactive to stress, pro-social, and less prone to addictive behaviors." Citizens in constant contact with law-enforcement may be proof of "**intergenerational transmission** of stress and adversity." Abused children are predisposed (brains are rewired) to experience anxiety, panic attacks and depression. Neglected and stressed pups grew up "timid, submissive, fearful, less gregarious, and more prone to depression and stress-sensitive disorders." Even essential hormones needed for brain development were lacking in the neglected and stressed pups. Stressed parents become negligent parents, who leave society and law-enforcement to discipline unruly and violent teens—social learning. Dr. Meaney found that maternal stress influences biological mechanisms, alters brain circuits and connections, structural and molecular changes that create behavioral changes—that last for several generations. Even neurotransmitters were altered, further influencing how adults abused as children, appraise situations and their own bodily sensations—especially their basic emotional reflex level.

PATTERNS, NERVE IMPULSES AND HORMONES

Neurodevelopmental disorders like anxiety, depression, schizophrenia and autism are believed to have developed during basic childhood brain changes. Many scientists have sounded the alarm over newborn cesarean delivery methods that bypass necessary vaginal microbiota. You are more likely to be overweight if you were born utilizing cesarean methods. Scientists found that gut microbial behavior can be made more aggressive and dangerous when the **stress hormone norepinephrine** was activated. You may believe you are responding appropriately to a stressful violent incident, but out of your awareness you may be producing dangerous amounts of the stress hormone corticosterone. Neuroscientist Bud Craig reminds us that "the purpose of every emotion is to maintain balance of the entire organism." Police-officers respond to various psycho-social influences, while their gut "responds to what they eat." Your body responds to your emotional state—which generates a feeling. How familiar are you with your "personal patterns of **emotional expression**," that further negatively influences your gut microbes, that further negatively (feedback loop) influences your mind-body—interkingdom signaling, especially motivational states and your sense-of-self. You may find your attention and awareness skills atrophy into **only recognizing negative stimuli**, not positive stimuli. Recent experiments indicate that your gut-brain axis also influences your REM sleep/dream states. Right now, how much does your gut-brain axis influence your background feeling state. How "unnatural" is your current diet for your lifestyle and health issues? Dr. Mayer describes just how much work your gut has to conduct, to keep you healthy. "Evolution has perfected the gut to sense, recognize, and encode everything we eat and drink into patterns of hormones and nerve impulses sent to regulatory centers in the brain." Do your eating habits make the job of your gut biome, even harder and less reliable?

CHAPTER FIVE
<u>NEGATIVE STATES OF MEMORY</u>

Police shootings are so rare and emotionally overpowering, that experts remind us that it is not uncommon to experience "tunnel hearing" and "tunnel vision," resulting in "tunnel memory." Perception of shooting-events may be recalled later with minor differences, total differences—or unrecognized by the experiencer. You may be intentionally and actively repressing your memory, or an aspect of mental-recall-paralysis. Experts describe that you may be so actively reliving (habitual patterns) the traumatic event in the here-and-now, that you are not actually using your memory to revive the trauma. You are actively (behavioral action) recreating the event over-and-over with or without memory awareness recall. Your post-reaction as the actual shooter, or witnessing the shooting, seems to become a blend of transitory distress that may become more persistent than you expected about yourself. Sometimes mental distress can become a disability. For some trauma victims, the memory is so over-powering and distracting, that the memory displaces actual in-the-moment sensory perception of real life. For law-enforcement, "trauma," is indicative of difficulties in "memory-processing" and emotional stress involving on-the-job horrible stimulus. Just when you think everything has gotten better, a **"reactivated memory"** entraps you back in negative states of memory—disordered consciousness. Do you have any **"conditioned-fear-responses?"** Creating automatic reactions and attitudes that become disturbed personalities and habitual reactions.

Trauma changes your mental processing skills and further negatively influences mental processes involving **memory reconsolidation and extinction**. Do you have an "injured nervous system" that requires a "neural prostheses." Memory reconsolidation is a "distinct molecular process," separate and distinct from memory consolidation—indicating the fragility of the process. You have absolutely vital molecular processes working alongside your neural processes. You do not just have neurochemical systems operating out of your awareness in your brain, but they are all "interrelated" and vital. Then we add pharmacological tampering and unhealthy lifestyles. Sadness modifies your brain, especially multiple cortex processes, and for some of us, requires an actual "voluntary-suppression" of sadness, which utilizes different cortex processes. Scientists do not seem to universally accept an identifiable division line between emotions and feelings. The two sides or hemispheres of your brain respond differently from each other involving induced emotions. How well do you know your personal "**dopamine-driven reward system**?" Do you have any "voluntary" control over your expression of negative emotions? If another police-officer described your "stereotypical emotional responses," what would be described. What is your definition of an "exuberant-temperament," and is it compatible with a job in law-enforcement? At what point does "behavior" become destructive? Some people can "drink-themselves-to-death," yet, live into their 60s and 70s. You can also practice intentionally creating healthier mental processes and other intended more-positive self-expressions. Self-directed neural-plasticity. Simple experience changes and alters your brain. Start now!

RELATING TO YOUR PAST

How familiar are you with your brain circuits that control "**motivation**?" Routine law-enforcement responses involving "anxiety-provoking fearful faces" may suddenly become complicated self-awareness. Symptoms, negative emotions and sensations of a physical nature activated by police-shootings can easily appear as minor distracting nuisances or posttraumatic reactions requiring a consciously intended response, instead of uncontrolled inappropriate and counterproductive behavior.

"**Trauma**" keeps a police-officer out of (direct-experience) the here-and-now. **PTSD** influences your ability to evaluate dangerous situations. Innocuous situations may be thought of as threatening in nature, or the police-officer misinterprets and turns the situation into a dangerous situation. It is hard to recognize as it happens, your "psychological" interference with proper memory formation and analysis. The physical "**imprints of trauma**" contaminating unmediated knowing, sensing, thoughts and perception. Investigations into chronic PTSD, revealed that brain/mental processes involving "self-awareness" and "body-awareness" have recessed in size because of less usage. Harm is compounded because those same reduced activity areas of the brain, are also involved in our socio-cultural feelings of connection, even basic feelings of joy and pleasure. This altered "way-you-remember" experience—is the biggest factor in how you "relate to your past."

Have you even considered "inventing new patterns of behavior?" PTSD, or simple depression, severely influences your ability to initiate "goal-seeking behaviors." It also infects your ability to participate in goal-directed activities—the successful outcome of which—does not matter to you. PTSD alters which "internal behavioral reinforcers" your subconscious places into the coveted "conscious awareness." "**Pain**" is not only sensory-awareness, it also involves emotional responses to the same stimulus. On a scale of 1 to 10, how accurate is your "perception-of-pain" in others? How about in yourself on a normal day. How about in yourself avoiding the diagnosis of PTSD? PTSD greatly reduces the chances for your emotional responses to contribute to a successful resolution. You have inner PTSD-expectations that change your normal responses to emotional or violent incidents you are dispatched to. Scientists also warn us that out of our knowledge of "positive emotional states," **happiness** is the one emotion that is "unclear," "ill-defined," and "least understood!" Is there a "genetic basis for happiness?" Emotions have neural correlates that are challenging to decipher, further complicated and shaded in natural variations from human to human. Do we investigate the personality or the environment. Diagnosing positive affective—**mood states**—is made more complicated by psychological evaluations that are more influenced by the "medical-experts" (quality-control issues) personal expectations, ambitions, feelings at that moment, personal training, timing, attention and distraction issues. Our over-confidence in dealing with complex emotional and violent incidents is over-shadowed by recognizing that the older parts of our brain process emotional behavior—self and other.

PROCEDURAL MEMORIES

FIXED-ACTION PATTERNS

Some experts believe that therapy for some traumatic events may require more than a verbal-psycho-analysis process. It may require actual physical recreation and physical action of the recreated stimulus event, to fully and permanently heal the patient. Perhaps calling a law-enforcement officer experiencing trauma, a "patient," could turn them off from the healing process. I felt a little bit like that just typing this part, disliking being considered a "patient." Do you have minor issues involving improper breathing and muscle tension—reflective self-awareness. That may be the slightest hint that you may have not fully resolved a previous traumatic experience. Traumatic survival memories may interfere with your standard procedural memories involved with "**learned motor actions**" and every potential emergency response you consider— especially issues of approach or withdrawal motivations for action. How aware are you of all your "**hidden-motivations?**" A "lingering-gaze" that you make for no identifiable reason, may be the first sign of an "emerging-memory" trying to get your attention, possibly an alert of danger detected out of your awareness. Perhaps a partial "implicit-trigger" memory you experienced was based on an insignificant (**relational context**) "sensorial-experience." We all have physiological access to our procedural memories, the sense of your physical body. A police-officers "fixed action patterns" influenced by his personal procedural memory determines the quality of his or her "emergency-based-survival" behavior—maladaptive or successful.

HYPER-AROUSAL OR HYPO-AROUSAL

Have you ever evaluated your instinctual "innate" reactive action patterns that will save your life before you even realize you are in danger? Some of our **"threat detections"** or perceptions of danger, can be based on the flimsiest superficial similarities and distracted awareness, as an interference or intuition that saves your life. When a group of police-officers respond to a dangerous incident, just observing one officer preparing for the potential of danger, automatically initiates similar preparation in others. Humans are hardwired (biological drive) to interpret serious and intense fear or anger emotional intensity, unconsciously, as a true assessment requiring immediate basic survival behaviors, even if based on false attributions based on false memories. Some shifts seem to keep us in a **"relaxed alertness" frame-of-mind**—for the whole shift and long-afterwards. Every one of us determines the "intensity" assessment of the situation, differently; hyperarousal or hypoarousal. It is your thoughts about the situation, especially adverse novel situations, that allow defense orienting sequences and prepared-motor-action processing to initiate, whether helpful or not. Traumatic memories whether accurate or not, create fixed-beliefs that may dominate your unconscious mental processing skills—especially future projection. Some therapists teach you how to **"renegotiate"** your traumatic memories as a major step in healing. Therapists can help you determine if you are in a "state-of-shutdown" or really are as calm as you appear to be.

Not all symptoms of **unresolved traumatic experience** issues are obvious overblown emotional displays. Traumatic events are not just "dangerous" events. My birth mother was a child-rapist. Forty plus years later, four particular autopsies I attended investigating murders and suspicious deaths, I still relive through mental images that I recall without intent. All the other autopsies I attended are "seemingly" lost from memory, just these four autopsies return all these years later. I had already witnessed dead bodies while living in Gary Indiana before I joined the Army. I had responded as a patrolman to vehicle accidents with fatalities. It may not be the "**autopsy**" part that I involuntarily remember them. Each one had a story that may have snagged some emotional issues deep in my head. The first one was at Fort Huachuca Arizona. A Korean-American housewife had consumed a bottle of prescription drugs, went out to a sports field, found a seldom used area, and died. She spent at least two days in the Arizona sun. At the autopsy, as the pathologist was prepared to enter the stomach for samples, the incision released a horrible greenish/blue gas-cloud that forced the pathologist to calmly yell "run!" He was not sure if the cloud was injurious to observers, so just to be safe, he had us leave temporarily. The cloud was so deeply colorful, it looked science-fiction. I had just spent two tours myself in Korea. Was that why I still remember the military housewife being cut open? In Frankfurt West Germany, I attended the autopsy of a military housewife who had just given birth and was jogging to lose the weight. She died on the track. By then, autopsies were second nature to me, so I do not think it was the autopsy part that I am having trouble letting go of. The military ambulance crew was told by dispatch that the patient had suffered a heart attack while jogging. The ambulance crew arrived and ran to the patient who was pretty far from the parking area, without defib or other equipment. One person had to run back to the ambulance and run back. When I tried to interview the ambulance crew, the medical doctors at the Army hospital blocked me and did everything they could do to get the crew out of the building. The medical unit refused to cooperate. That may be what part of the autopsy that I have been unable to let go of.

The third autopsy occurred at Fort Gordon Georgia, involving an eleven-year-old dependent boy of an Army Staff Sergeant (SSG). The SSG had lost his temper and threw his boy across a room into a rock/cement fireplace. I do not think it was the autopsy part of this incident that I still recall decades later. My real father's favorite way to punish me until I could fight back, was picking me up off the ground by choking my neck and bashing the back of my head into the wall. Seeing this 11-year-old kid, dead, looking so skinny, like he was only six years old, my childhood memories resonated with this incident. The fourth autopsy involved a six-month-old baby. Returning from out west, the parents had drove 26 hours straight, with the baby in the back seat—while both chain-smoked cigarettes all the way back to Fort Gordon. The draft synopsis of my investigation clearly identified that I believe the nicotine cigarette poisoning of the baby was the cause of death. I found out later, when the report required my signature, that the "Chief-of-Investigations" had deleted all my mentioning of the cigarette-cause-effect = death summary. This bothered me at the time, I was furious that this chain-smoking supervisor deleted the cigarette aspects and blamed "sudden-infant-death" syndrome. He, like me, had worked many years working primarily drug-investigations, resulting in about half of our arrests, involving zero-death capitalist marijuana consumers. A hundred-thousand plus deaths involving tobacco are ignored for the prized tax-revenue. If you are lucky enough to be alive four decades after your last law-enforcement mission, you may be surprised by what past experience of yours, invades pleasantly or unpleasantly, into your old age. Experts warn that all your law-enforcement **subjective experience memory—has a "bodily component."**

LAW-ENFORCEMENT PROFESSIONAL ALLEGIANCE

Simple human-second-guessing can become a mental block that keeps you forever out of the here-and-now. In law-enforcement, we may not have all the time necessary to evaluate and implement a decision. When we **make a decision**, it helps our mental-health to believe that decision was the right thing to do. Doubt will enter with or without your permission. It is one thing to believe other police-officers at the scene agreed with your decision to shoot, and quite another thing if other police-officers want to hear about it over-and-over, whether you want to discuss it or not. Mental health experts remind us how important the views, interpretations and attitudes of the other police officers, help determine the mental-health recovery of the officer who fired the weapon. A dangerous emotional incident with multiple police-officers responding requires all responding-officers to understand each other; their specific individual skills for these kinds of incidents, and their decision-making preferences and attitudes. It takes the right kind of leadership for paramilitary organizations like law-enforcement to remain impartial, honest, not seeking out revenge and always seeking the truth. You may be full of "natural-strengths," physical and mental, but if you never get to utilize them on the job, you may become less-satisfied with your job. Being a different professional than you expected to become, may also cause you to leave law-enforcement. It is not uncommon for police-officers to totally lose their **personal off-duty identity** in favor of their "police-identity." Your personal identity has been replaced by what you "identify-with," and all the attachments that come with that identity. Can you really separate your identity with what you identify with? What is the "message" that your life has revealed so far? The cultural assumptions and stories you tell yourself deep in your mind, create expectations and judgments that limit your potential in law-enforcement. Take responsibility for the stories you tell yourself, or change them immediately. Recognizing doubt and other hidden forces can be the first step for improving your personal and professional control issues. Your imagination may be revealing more about yourself, to yourself, than any feedback from family and friends. Your imagination, like anxiety, may be recognized as a "rehearsal of fear." Are you really so busy—that you don't have time for some healthy self-reflection and self-healing? Does your imagination rehearse a lack of empathy incompatible for law-enforcement, locking your intention in negativity and self-pity? You are more than your allegiance to your professional choice in law-enforcement. Your emotional patterns and behavior will reveal more about yourself and what you identify with, than all the verbal descriptions and perspectives you provide others. Your "way-of-seeing" (relationship and experience) is not set in stone and can always be improved upon. In law-enforcement, your choices effect, affect and infect the citizens we interact with. Is our personal "mentalese" just an intolerable distraction that keeps us in uncertainty and disappointment.

REFLECTIVE AWARENESS OR ROBOTIC ANTICIPATION

The police-trainer, who while training a rookie, pulled her real pistol, yelled taser-taser-taser and shot and killed a driver, had a very interesting interaction immediately after the shooting, with another police-officer. He offered to exchange his gun with her gun, recognizing the evidentiary value of securing the weapon. I do not know if this is common nowadays? It seemed to keep her calm and focused on him, while he gently got her weapon. I have always expected that a police-officer who shot and killed someone, not physically wounded or injured himself, should be emotionally secure enough to be interviewed as soon as possible. Some experts report that this may not always be the case. Personal feelings of anticipation, flavored by your habits, reactions, beliefs and expectations, may easily become "**anticipatory-obedience**," that you energized; may not reach your conscious "reflection" awareness. Robotic anticipation instead of de-escalation behavioral responses to the situation you find yourself in. Institutional loyalty and obedience without hesitation or evaluation. Regular average policemen in Germany, murdered more Jewish and other "undesirable" citizens, than were murdered in concentration camps. Cognitive experiments have investigated different theories involving the "**forming-of-beliefs**." Do you believe you already carry every possible or potential belief in your mind that you "believe?" Or, do your "beliefs" not really exist until you are asked or triggered to recognize you possess a particular "belief?" How about your "intentions" in life. Do all your intentions already exist in your mind, and it is just the "moment" that activates and reveals your proper intention? Are all of your "intentions" based on "beliefs" that have been verified as applicable to your in-that-moment behavioral response? Evaluate your own personal experience of mood. Are you proud of your "moods?" A confident attitude-judgment that just-seems-right, will make you more confident that your decision was correct, even if it was not correct or helpful. Your attitude and behavior, whether intended or not, has consequences (personal and professional) that you are responsible for—especially how you treat other people. Personal awareness can be your greatest teacher, or trap you in old behavior.

CHAPTER SIX

ATTITUDE JUDGMENT DECISION MAKING

The standard description of mental processes involved with human thought are now being considered thru a new quantum-mathematical theory. Experts identify the old paradigm concerning human thought mental processes as based on antiquated probabilistic models that served as an important initial starting point, but quantum descriptions they believe are more definitive and informative. **Are all "decisions" merely a form of "judgment?"** How many judgment-decision categorical thought processes do you make out of conscious awareness? Are all these different judgment-decisions "entangled" (quantum correlations) like quantum processes are? Are these judgment-decisions so entangled that they are not really separate processes or subsystems? The "sure thing principle" is an aspect of **"decision-theory**." Some of the more important "perception" aspects of law-enforcement are routinely initially analyzed out of our awareness, a never-ending flow of "judgment" processes involving uncertainty and certainty. Simply changing your point of attention from one person to another is quite an inner neurological journey, requiring multiple brain-processes that operate out of your awareness. What is the quality of your never-ending routine-patrol "attitude-judgments," both yours and the citizens you are interacting with—a circular attention and awareness interpretive multidimensional dance? Do you see your thought-cognitive processes as similar to "particle" standard physics descriptions, or more as the quantum—wave "indefinite" thought processing "potential."

PROBABILITIES—YOU EXPECT TO EXPECT

This quantum mechanical theory attempts to "modernize" long-held beliefs concerning human thought processes. Not necessarily replacing "probabilistic models," but introducing quantum mathematical theories as a way to describe thought processes from a "quantum interaction" aspect influencing decision-making thought process. Decision making mental cognitive processing bathed in **"interference" and "uncertainty;"** (preferences, bias, beliefs) may require unconscious "contextual" issues to be clarified or reviewed—potentially utilizing this quantum-mathematical thought theory. A police-officer at a crime scene, may experience "interference" and "uncertainty," unaware, if the situation, or personal internal-mentalese is the cause. Do you allow your mind to lead your thoughts astray? Do your thoughts lead your mind astray? Do you have no control? How much of your decision-making is based on **pre-structured beliefs and programming**, or the opposite, **at-that-moment "psychological intuition?"** This was bound to happen, when "cognitive scientists" and "decision scientists" schemed together with "quantum scientists." Quantum investigations into the science of "observation," are closely linked to quantum entanglement, where key moments involved with simple "observation" or "measurement" create and entangle the "observer" with the "observed." Scientists pointed out that their version of thought-quantum-mathematical theories did not tackle "quantum-mind" processes, which I hope somebody does.

Review **"double-slit"** physics videos on the internet involving how a photon shot from a single position, can "switch" from particle existence to a wave existence striking two detectors instead of just one. Procedural interplay and observation "changes and transforms its objects." It is why I believe **"consciousness"** (deliberate intention) is as fundamental to our universe, as time and space. "Pre-existing" properties that seem to not exist until the activity of "measurement" observation requires their existence in our experiments—in our dimension, in our world? Both the quantum scientist and the police-officer on routine patrol searching for **"primary-data,"** assign or determine "probabilities" to their professional "events" experience. Your pre-existing neural-architecture determines what "probabilities" you **expect to expect,** even if such expectations have nothing to do with the reality of the situation you have responded to. If de-escalation potential is not part of your "belief" expectations and pre-programming, it won't even enter your mental self-talk personal experience. "Causal-closure" beliefs are utilized by the physicist and the police-officer. Law-enforcement investigate physical acts of violence on physical human-beings, locate a suspect, "case-causal-closed." Some scientists believe that only "physical properties" are able to act on the "physical world"; consciousness as subjective experience does not act on the physical world, "consciousness-causal-case closed!" I disagree, but most of the experts I research, do not believe consciousness is fundamental to our universe.

Every human emits their private **electro-magnetic-signature,** not in the traditional (electric company) standard power-level that remains constant; but, in "discrete packets of energy." Observation and measurement that influences potential realities, are as difficult and complicated to document, as quantum-data—even simple location and momentum interference-pattern analysis can activate quantum phenomena into actual-value "existence." Dr. Jeffrey M. Schwartz describes a version of the "double-slit" experiment that used "ions," like the ions your neurons utilize for "action-potential" communication. Dr. Schwartz described "ions" in a way that science-fiction writers will carry their next plot: "Ions are subject to all of the counterintuitive rules of quantum physics." Ions are also key to **"triggering neurotransmitter release**," a major contributor to police-officers losing control of their own behavior. Every police-officer begins their patrol flavored or poisoned by all their unconscious private personal baggage of pre-programmed "waves-of-probability" expectations and resulting self/other superpositions and entanglement. Do you have any **off-duty interests**, or are you all police—24-hours a day. No friends outside of law-enforcement? Time for a hobby, and with the internet you can determine for yourself the potential quantum-revolution influence on police-sciences, before someone explains it at you and for you. YouTube has wonderful videos related to quantum research; just verify your sources and their motivations.

OBSERVATIONAL BEHAVIORAL INFLUENCE

My research of one particular investigation into **"thought-quantum-theory**," required mathematical formula symbolism for mental processes that I did not buy-into. I read their 400+page book and was not very impressed. In 2024, most experts all seem to agree that we do not understand quantum theory enough—to claim we do. When theoretical physics investigations read more like "philosophy." Do not get frightened by the mathematics, I still enjoy reading quantum-subjects and I barely understand algebra. Police recognize **"hidden-variables"** in their field-of-vision, and Einstein saw **"hidden-variables"** in the physical world—both investigations seeking "certainties" based on (determinism?) what we-do-know. Investigating the unknown, utilizing the known. Somehow our jails became "mental-institutions" where "two coexisting parallel mental realities" in forced interaction, barely tolerate each other. Not good for community, citizen or police-officer. Classic physics coexisting within quantum physics? Explain phenomenon that was never observed, during a science lecture, or worse, during courtroom testimony. Many targets of scientific investigation cannot be observed or actually detected; science observes what is around the target, and the behavioral influence the original target has on what little we can observe, just like the police-officer. Your act of observation may improperly influence the experiment. Dr. Schwartz describes the nervous-awareness he had the first time he used **"mental-force"** in a manuscript—implying this force not merely symbolic. Posing questions is the investigative beginning for scientist and police-officer. Has quantum-mechanics erased any belief that the conscious-mind is separate from matter? Do neurons explain everything?

No job is enjoyable when you are in pain, especially in law-enforcement dealing with aches and pains while you may have to wrestle someone into cuffs or chase them down. Contrary to most of our expectations, aspirin once ingested, does not proceed straight to your brain. Instead, your "inflammatory-response" is modified concerning your "free nerve endings," that would normally be sending pain-messages to your brain. **Aspirin blocks** "prostaglandins," which would normally sensitize free nerve endings in the injured area and alert the brain of injury "pain." The injured area is still in need of attention, just the minds pain-interpretation alert-system is altered. Everybody experiences pain differently when your mind is the primary judge and jury for "pain" issues, more so, than the actual injured area.

"The Brain-gut-microbiota axis." Experts remind us that not only do humans have constant on-going bidirectional communication (including mood and appetite), between our brain and gut, but that gut microbes weigh about as much as our brain. Gut microbe cells outnumber human cells by ten to one. Gut bacteria synthesize cytokines, neuromodulators and neurotransmitters important for daily functioning. The "Vagus nerve" is vitally important in this bidirectional communication. Western medicine seems to neglect the importance of the Vagus nerve and the enteric nervous system. Gut microbes are believed to be the source of a protein, pathogens or toxins that travels up the Vagus nerve (not the bloodstream) increasing the risk for developing Parkinsons Disease. The science of "psychobiotics," probiotic bacteria believed to provide mental health benefits, seems to benefit patients suffering depression and anxiety. Some disturbances of body functions are termed "psychosomatic" illnesses. Emotional factors such as pending divorce or incompatibility and stress involving work issues, are believed to contribute to psychosomatic illnesses. The brain-gut microbiota axis may be influenced by your gut-bacteria experiencing psychosomatic illnesses that you detect, but assume it's all in your head. Your ancient brain structure referred to as the "old-brain," is your primary source for unconscious healthy functioning homeostatic operations. Your old-brain works out of your conscious awareness along with your brain-gut microbiota axis, what could go wrong? Your old-brain communicates with your new brain every time you experience pain and fatigue messages.

EXHAUSTION SENSORY DISCONNECT

(**The Sleeping Brain**). There are many theories concerning just why humans need "sleep." Normal evolutionary processes should have developed an alternative to "sleep," because it puts the sleeping human or animal in such a weak (sensory disconnection) dangerous situation. Outside stimuli signaling a threat may be missed or delayed while sleeping. Simple sleep deprivation can negatively infect your awareness and attention skills, especially risk assessment for law-enforcement duties. An exhausted police-officer usually does not communicate efficiently and effectively. Homeostatic regulation is on-going and functions primarily at the subconscious level. For sleep to require "sensory disconnection," means that some important function or process must occur during sleep. I learned how to experience "lucid-dreaming," the ability to take charge of my dreams if I so choose, in high-school. Routinely, I find myself remembering these lucid dreams, occasionally trying to determine if my memory is of a dream or a real-life situation. One theory of "synaptic renormalization" details that during sleep, our brain consolidates the days memories more energized and directed by your "overall knowledge," than the dream message itself. I taught myself "lucid-dreaming" many years ago to play in my dreams instead of being hostage to childhood trauma and military issues. Many experts describe that when elderly patients stop seeking "fun," this is considered potential indicators of mental deterioration.

Most law-enforcement agencies try to equip their police-officers with the most up-to-date and current equipment, vehicles, training and BOLO type information dissemination. The importance of **officer safety** is stressed daily before we begin our next shift. While your agencies policies may influence your mood and attitude, you remain the biggest factor in your own mood and attitude toward law-enforcement duty and citizen-interaction. Was law-enforcement the right choice of employment for you? While you "routine-patrol" and gather information in your assigned area, your gut is also gathering information about your food intake, food desires, and your environment every millisecond. Your family life, or neighbor relationships are obvious factors in your health, happiness and well-being. One aspect I believe is extremely important for law-enforcement, and yet, rarely ever considered; your "brain-gut-microbiome axis." Most of us were "programmed" food-preferences as a child, and are still subject to their unconscious influence on us. The communication (out of your awareness) between your brain-mind and your gut-microbiome is more complicated than you ever imagined. Is your law-enforcement career being negatively influenced by what Dr. Emeran Mayer called "**disturbances of brain-gut interaction**." The biggest factor influencing your mood and attitude may simply be your "mind-gut connection" signaling molecules as chemical conversations. I recommend Dr. Mayers book, "The Mind-Gut connection." It changed my attitude toward nutritional consumption and how the food I eat, may be the primary influencer on my "citizen-interaction."

HOMEOSTASIS-SENSORY PROTECTION

Every "emotion" you experience while on patrol, is mirrored in your gastrointestinal tract. This is a "coordinated-response" to what you feel, what Dr. Mayer called "a theatre in which the drama of emotion plays out." Not all intestinal tumors and inflammation can be easily detected by endoscopy. Not all **stress and threats** (genetically coded emotional operating systems) that a police-officer experiences during a shift, are recognized consciously. What unconscious or subconsciously detected threats are wreaking havoc (**stress molecules**) on your gut health? How often during a routine shift does your brain's emotional circuits (stress program) influence or shut down your digestive system because of stress or threats perceived—just to redirect or save energy? How often does your amygdala trigger fears and anxieties? Future expectations, circumstances and simple memories can negatively influence your gut-biome. The power of your gut-biome can even cause your stomach to "empty its contents upward," including hydrochloric acid that can damage your esophagus. Simple emotional mental disturbances can disturb or inhibit properly functioning brain-gut interaction, the sensory information of which 90%, never reaches your conscious awareness. Your over-all health is heavily influenced by your gut-biome—especially their search for "hostile intruders." The goal of your neurobiological search for "homeostasis," is self-protection—autonomic, neuroendocrine, and behavioral functions guided by thermoregulation energy efficiency (homeostatic valuation). Your brain may prioritize thermoregulatory behavioral motivation, at the expense of other bodily functions—optimal energy utilization.

Neuroscientist A.D. (Bud) Craig's book, How Do You Feel is very technical, but well worth reading, especially how he developed his "homeostatic model of awareness." Craig explains that he discusses "awareness," instead of "consciousness," "because the latter can't be defined." How much of your behavior, interoceptive signals and awareness is motivated, controlled and guided by emotional motivations and feelings? Craig describes that "**all of our behaviors are emotional behaviors.**" Behavior patterns that you exhibit, are genetically heritable. Do you recognize any adaptive behaviors or fixed action patterns that you inherited from your family? It is likely that autonomic activation of your emotional behaviors actually precedes (precognitively), your recognition or awareness that your emotional behavior has changed. A predictive mechanism (action-specific-values) that you may not be aware of is your mental "as-if-loop." Your ability to mentally model, even out of your awareness, behavioral options and their specific associated feelings anticipated. Do you interpret your feelings as the "cause" of your behavior, or the "consequence of behavior."

EMOTIONAL ANALYSIS—BIDIRECTIONAL SIGNALING

Dr. Mayer reminds us that the largest sensory organ of your body— is your gut—when spread out it is "the size of a basketball court." Even low-grade inflammation caused by gut disturbances, can contribute to "obesity, heart disease, chronic pain, and degenerative diseases of the brain." Your gut communicates "gut sensations" to your brain, where emotional analysis is communicated back to your gut—**bidirectional signaling**. Dr. Mayer called this "the most efficient language that to this day supports all life on Earth." Your brain-gut connective "feelings" are not the same as your "reactions." Your gut may even influence your "**police-intuition**" skills. The quality of your gut microbial diversity is believed to contribute to neurodevelopmental disorders and neurodegenerative disorders. One estimate is that only 10% of the cells in or on your body, are human—over 1000 bacterial species. The next time you are hungry, stop and think whose hunger are you trying to satisfy, your gut biome or your human-centric "sense-of-self." While we may consider ourselves human, "super-organisms," we are really "supra-organisms," with our microbial shared biological interconnectedness eco-system that we cannot live without.

Recognizing that a co-worker in law-enforcement is experiencing **depression issues**, can be hard when your interaction is dictated by emotionally charged sometimes violent incidents. Depression has been "cured" by simple fecal matter transfer from another person who is not depressed. Clinical studies have proven that you can make a person depressed simply by fecal matter transfer from a depressed person. The biggest influence on the severity and duration of your depression, may not be pharmaceuticals or therapy, but your gut-health. Law-enforcement not only routinely behave in human-species-specific adaptive behaviors, but we also have law-enforcement-species-specific adaptive behaviors. The first time you experience a long-foot-pursuit (exercise pressor reflex), and the extreme difficulty of getting cuffs on someone who is not as out-of-breath as you, you should consider **nutritional changes** to your diet, in addition to working out more (vasoreceptive feedback). Your aortic chemoreceptors are alerting you that your carbon dioxide levels exceed normal ongoing regulation of respiration depth—chemosensory modulation of respiratory activity and ongoing thermoregulation. Neuropeptide release will help maintain tissue integrity—vascular system feedback. If you safely can, you will be motivated to initiate unconsciously, recuperative withdrawal behaviors. Bud Craig amusingly reminds us that: "In both worms and humans, there are homeostatic sensory fibers which signal safety instead of danger." Your hypothalamus will guide you during aggressive and defensive behavioral activity even while bathed in emotional intensity and escape behavior— **sympathoexcitation and motor preparatory responses**. Your entire shift will require interoceptive integration of your feelings and facial feedback—assisted by your interoceptive cortex, engendering homeostatic sentience.

STRESS RESPONSE

PSYCHOLOGICAL/PHYSIOLOGICAL/NEURO-GENESIS

"Emotionally significant visual activity" still requires that visual stimulus to reach your awareness. Law-enforcement may have more "preautonomic command signals" (experienced behavioral value) than the citizens we interact with—anticipation anxiety-emotional significance and high-quality social communication. Your behavioral level of motivations is always influenced by your emotional maturity. Most American doctors are not well trained in providing "evidence-based nutritional advice." We were prescribed antibiotics to the point that the targets of these more powerful antibiotics, were becoming "immune" to these antibiotics— dysbiosis. These more powerful antibiotics kill the unintended, as well as the intended—especially in your gut. The medical community considered the "collateral damage" from powerful antibiotics (machine model) as unfortunate, but acceptable. Our medical journals that used to keep pharmaceutical giants relatively honest, are now controlled by these same pharmaceutical giants. We may have the most **expensive health care** in the world, but it is disappointingly very low statistically in relation to performance and level of health care quality for American citizenry. Modern "profit-driven" food-chain issues have negatively influenced the health of the average American. Poor eating habits influence just how much serotonin you naturally create in your brain, especially the biochemistry of the child's developing brain. **"Neurogenesis"** is not a Star Trek movie—it is the birth of neurons, synapse connections and the development and maintenance of electrochemical networks. Proteins are synthesized and neurotransmitters need to "bind." Stabilized synapses require long-term potentiation, a process that is easily and negatively interrupted. Health influences behavioral issues. Many times, we simply treat the symptoms, not the cause. The **"physiology" of your stress response** is just as influential and important as your psychological health. I believe our "not-for-profit" health-care system is controlled by profiteers—who would rather see Americans not eat healthy. Ultimately, many approved prescription medications require constant monitoring to determine when side-effects and other issues, make the value of the perceived benefits—questionable.

PSYCHIATRIC DISORDERS MAY HAVE A BIOLOGICAL BASIS

You may recognize the mind-body connection personally, but if your doctor does not have the time to help you improve your mind-body connection, they will usually rely on pharmaceuticals as a catch-all solution. Your digestive system is "intricately connected" (enteric nervous system) with your brain (microbe speak), to the point that your gut-biome is a major influence on your basic emotional health. Your brain signals to your gut your emotional status, brain-gut-microbiome—a "single integrated system." Are you aware when your gut prolongs negative emotional states? Your **emotional regulating centers** may be negatively influenced by poor gut-health. Decision making, temperament and even social interactions are heavily influenced by your guts emotional influence. When we consider our immune system, we are quick to assume that our blood and bone marrow is where most of our immune cells reside. Actually, **more immune cells reside in your gut**. 95% of the serotonin in your body is stored in your gut. Diversity and abundance are the key for your normal healthy gut microbiota and mental well-being. Gut-microbes influence your "appetite-control" system, more than your own will-power. Many major psychiatric disorders have a biological basis.

DESCRIBE THE DIFFERENCE BETWEEN <u>OBSERVED PHENOMENON</u> AND <u>UNOBSERVED PHENOMENON</u>

This book is intended for military, law-enforcement, prosecutors and even defense attorneys. I am aware that this group is most guilty of reading copies of books, especially unauthorized copied E-books, that leave the author unpaid. Please pay for this book.

Even though I was "Regular-Army" for over a decade, I did not qualify for any retirement plans when I chose to leave the Army in 1987. After four overseas tours with the Army, I was advised that I would be taking over another CID Drug Suppression Team, this time stateside. This was expected, as I did have a DEA diploma. I did not like being ordered to arrest soldiers for marihuana and hashish, while Army policies deterred me from targeting investigations specific to the Army's horrible (yet-condoned) prescription drug-abuse epidemic after America's war in Vietnam. Alcohol abuse created most of the "problems" that my years in the Military Police needed to respond to. During basic-training, our "C-rations" included three cigarettes in each meal, that was how old these meals were. Alcoholic drunkenness as ignored compensation for the hard life of a post-Vietnam soldier. With budgets cuts after the war in Vietnam, we were paid like crap, promoted hardly at all, housed like crap, advance training budgets dried up, pay-raises almost non-existent, supplied like crap, etc.... Congressional investigations into the Vietnam War determined that the reason we did not get public support for the war, was because mostly Regular Army soldiers were sent, and nobody really missed them. It was determined that if we sent more National Guard and Reservists centered in certain areas, the people would be more aware of their deployment and appreciate their mission. Congressional investigations had to find a" scapegoat" other than we should not have been involved in Vietnam's civil war—to begin with.

Twice, as a CID Special Agent, I was involved with a surprise inspection of military pharmacies, and both times, just as I was finding discrepancies, I was advised to leave because my presence was making pharmacists nervous and uneasy, which might cause a medication error. So many times, when I would inform the commander of a soldier that I bought marihuana/hashish from, they would reply that he was "one of my best soldiers." I am talking over half of the time. There were times when a commander would be thrilled because the soldier I "titled' in a drug-investigation deserved to be kicked out of the Army a long-time ago. There were times when a commander chose not to punish the soldier for selling me marihuana because the soldier was a such a good soldier. Per CID-SOP, I had to go over the commanders' head, to battalion, brigade levels—sometimes to General Staff. Now adays, government departments seeking computer technicians for jobs in the "intelligence-field" are being told to ignore any marihuana use and arrests, as "computer-geeks" are uninterested in a job where they get tested for marihuana. I chose to get out of the Army when I was told I was being forced to take another Team Chief position with a CID Drug Suppression Team. I was only nine-years from retirement eligibility, but I could not live with myself, if I continued prioritizing marihuana related investigations.

I had signed up originally in 1976 for the Military Police with a guaranteed first assignment in Korea, since Vietnam was no longer an option. I signed up at the beginning of my senior year of high-school in 1976, because that was the last year for the Vietnam era benefits package. By the time I arrived in Korea as an Army MP, I was told that the Army had made a mistake. They did not intend to qualify soldiers who were "inactive-reserve" in 1976, for Vietnam era benefits. To qualify for MP school, I had to get a high-school diploma first. If I did not get my high-school diploma, I would go to Infantry school instead. That is how I ended up with no benefits after a decade of Regular Army and four overseas tours.

After the Army, I worked for the Lake County IN Sheriff's department in their Community Corrections section. I was recruited because it was expanding and the "intentions" of Community Corrections work-release programs allowing the poor and middle class to keep their jobs and keep supporting their families—appealed to me. After five years I realized how every position was politically controlled and dependent on a few politicians of both major parties. I refused to show up at political events as foot soldiers for certain politicians. I would get no promotions or pay-raises until I "played-the-game." During this time the Chief of Detectives for the Lake County Sheriff's department was arrested for corruption, including frequently driving his son to certain business areas for the purpose of his son robbing a business, then escaping with his father in his detective's vehicle. The Sheriff was arrested for some kind of tow-truck scheme.

My very first week with community corrections, I was verbally reprimanded for insisting on obtaining a urine-sample from a jail-trustee, who had earned a day out in the community with his family. I then realized that the work-release portion of Community Corrections was designed in favor of higher-paid white-collar criminals, like dozens of lawyers, and executives. Poor and middle-class prisoners with low-paying jobs and one-check away from their families becoming homeless did not prop-up statistical success—as determined by income totals over actual help for the poor and middle class. Low-paying jobs did not help with the "statistical" evidence of the value of work-release Community Corrections. They needed those large salaries to show success. Most lawyers would submit a "work-schedule" claiming they were needed at their office from 8am to 8pm, six-days a week. Our surprise checks on them at their office revealed they would be napping, or with their girl-friends, rarely with a client. We were ordered to ignore this.

We had a "celebrity" working as staff in our Community Corrections office. He was known as an original guitarist or bassist for the Jackson 5, when they still lived in Gary. He had a lawsuit over copyright issues with Michael Jackson in a decades-long litigation effort. There was a video of him playing with the Jackson 5. He had a "scam" with new prisoners and staff, where he would promise to double their money, if they "loaned" him money in advance of the lawsuit he was definitely going to win—someday! He may have deserved the money from the Jackson 5, but he had no business using his position to solicit monies from prisoners and new-staff. What finally made me want to leave the job, was when a wannabe gangster resident, started openly dating a female Community Corrections employee. She even allowed him into our office, with door closed and allowed him to review prisoner and staff files. She was politically connected and protected, so these questionable behaviors were ignored. I had to leave that job before I would get caught-up in these questionable and illegal activities.

MILITARY SERVICE

FORT MCCLELLAN ALABAMA—**Basic training, Military Police school, Nuclear Security school, CID Special Agent Course**. *(While at Nuclear Security school, IRAN took our embassy staff hostage. Any Military Police in any school at Fort McClellan who had experience in Vietnam or Korea, were pulled from class and began emergency desert warfare training for our attempt that failed to rescue the hostages.)

CAMP AMES (CHONG-DONG-NI) KOREA—**110th Military Police** (Tower-jockeys, Tower-rats, Chairborne-Rangers) Worst duty I had as an MP, but this MP company had the highest (unit) "morale" and acceptance of death when compared to the rest of my assignments.

FORT BLISS TEXAS—**591st Military Police** (Patrolman, then Desk Sergeant). Guarded the Space-Shuttle Columbia during its visit to Biggs Army Airfield—we had 16 bomb threats. Also went to Fort Irwin outside Death Valley California for desert-warfare exercise.

CAMP CASEY (TONG-DU-CHONG) KOREA—**2nd Military Police**, 2nd Infantry Division. (Traffic-accident investigator and AWOL apprehension.)

FORT HUACHUCA ARIZONA—**CID Drug Suppression Team**, (Military Police Investigator).

CAMP KING WEST GERMANY—**570th Military Police** (Railway Military Police-European Theatre)

FRANKFURT WEST GERMANY—**CID Frankfurt Resident Agency** (Special Agent).

FORT GORDON GEORGIA—**CID Fort Gordon** (Special Agent).

Our official "motto" for the 110th MP in Korea was "The Wildmen of the Mountain."

Our official "motto" for CID was "Do What Has to be Done."

OTHER LAW-ENFORCEMENT AND MILITARY SCHOOLS: DEA school, Non-Commissioned Officers Academy, FBI Hostage Negotiation School, Child Abuse and Exploitation Investigation Techniques, Advanced Protective Services—Bodyguard Course, Narcotics Investigation Course, Defense Property Disposal Investigations Course, Fraud Detection Course, Drug Suppression Training Course, Emergency Vehicle Operations Course, etc.

TWO EXAMPLES CONCERNING HOW LOW MILITARY BUDGETS BECAME AFTER THE AMERICAN WAR IN VIETNAM:

1) While I was working Desk Sergeant duties (1978-1980) at the Fort Bliss Texas MP Station, the Provost Marshal sought volunteers for a mass-vehicle-traffic-ticketing campaign at nearby White Sands Missile Range. The judge at White Sands had determined that the MP traffic-tickets they issued for speeding were not reliable anymore, because they used the "pacing a certain distance following in their patrol-vehicles" method in order to determine their speed. The budget for the MPs at White Sands did not have any funds to replace their now broken speed radar-guns. Their budget could not be used for repairing their speed radar-guns. Once

210

word of the judge's decision spread around White Sands, military members still tried to abide by speed limits. Civilian workers and civilian contractors, though, took advantage of the situation and started speeding everywhere on post. The PROVOST MARSHAL was not happy. Fort Bliss Military Police drove up in our patrol-cars and old-fashioned MP Harley-Davidsons—with more than enough speed-radar devices to swamp the entire post. We were instructed that we could not re-fill our patrol vehicles with fuel at White Sands, their budget was so-low. At first the White Sands community were not aware that a different group of MPs were now patrolling their community, and they did not want to stop. We had to play bumper-cars with many civilian drivers on post. Desk Sergeants at the MP station at Fort Bliss were switched to twelve-hour shifts, so I stopped driving up to White Sands. The ticket-blitz worked.

2) When I was a CID Agent in Frankfurt, West Germany, I was ordered to Rhein Main Air Force Base, to obtain some very sensitive property from a pilot flying in from Berlin. Fortunately, I tested our crime-scene camera in-advance, which revealed the flash-batteries were spent. I went to CID supply and I was told that they have not been able to get batteries for our flash-attachments for a while. I drove to every PX and mini-PX anywhere near Frankfurt to purchase the batteries with my own money. I was going to have to take photos of evidence that would be reviewed by President Reagan. I met the pilot when he taxied to my location. He was nervous because I was in plain-clothes. I was Team Chief of the Drug Suppression Team and looking pretty rough. He asked for more ID than just my CID Credentials which did have my picture, but it was probably the first time he had ever seen CID Credentials. I pulled out my official Military ID and my civilian Indiana driver's license. This caused more confusion for him, because

coincidentally, I had been working on a case where I had a military informant who was, with my government funds, purchasing blank military ID cards from a civilian working at the Military Personnel Center, who was illegally selling them. I had a wallet full of blank military ID cards waiting to be documented on an evidence form. Once I explained why, he reluctantly handed me the important items. It was the clothing of a US Army Major who was shot on the East German side of our border. Under an agreement (SOFA— Status of Forces Agreement) with the Soviets; both countries had members of the other side allowed access to patrol along the border. This would show each side that neither side was massing troops along the border for a surprise war. The clothing of a deceased US Army Major was to be photographed by me, the photos of which were supposed to of been sent to the White House for review by President Reagan. Then, Military Intelligence wanted the clothing checked for fragments of the projectile that killed the Major, because it was supposed to be a new type of ammunition being used by the Warsaw Pact.

THE FOLLOWING AUTHORS, DOCTORS AND SCIENTISTS MAY BE SURPRISED TO FIND THAT I INCORPORATED IDEAS AND INFORMATION FROM THEIR BOOKS, INTO A BOOK DESIGNED TO IMPROVE POLICE-CITIZEN INTERACTION AND CITIZEN-POLICE INTERACTION:

Dr. James Allen, Mahzarin R. Banaji, Cognitive Scientist Dr. John Bargh, Cognitive Neuroscientist William H. Calvin, Neuroscientist Bud Craig, Author Stephanie Dowrick, Dr. William Glaser, Anthony G. Greenwald, Author Jonah Lehrer, Dr. Emeran Mayer, Neuroendocrinologist Bruce McEwan, Author David McRaney, Neuroscientist Michael

Meaney, Police Psychologist Laurence Miller, Neurobiologist Donald W. Pfaff, Scientist Jeffrey M. Schwartz, Dr. Michael Shermer, Psychiatrist Philip Tetlock, and Researcher Bob Zajong. Many-many thanks.

Made in the USA
Columbia, SC
21 March 2024

33170616R00124